THE CHOYCE LET

May and Arthur Jee's wedding at Portishead in April 1914. From left to right: Rev. John Coley Choyce, Eleanor Choyce (*née* Moxon), Eleanor 'Louie' Choyce, May Jee (*née* Choyce), Arthur Jee, Ralph Jee (Arthur's brother), Etheldred Jee (*née* Moxon – Arthur's mother and Louie's aunt), Thomas 'Tom' Choyce

THE
CHOYCE LETTERS™

Beatrix Potter to Louie Choyce
1916 - 1943

EDITED BY JUDY TAYLOR

The Beatrix Potter Society
London

LOUIE CHOYCE

Eleanor Louisa Choyce, or 'Louie' as she was always known by the family, was born in 1876, the eldest of the five children of Benjamin Coley Choyce and Eleanor Jane Moxon. On her mother's side Louie was a first cousin of my father, and her younger sister May married my uncle, Arthur Jee, so that I am related to Louie on two counts.

May and Arthur had a farm at Old Sodbury, then in Gloucestershire, where as children we used to spend our summer holidays before the Second World War, and where we lived for a time during the war. I would occasionally see Louie on the rare times our visits coincided. As I was less than ten at the time my memory of her is sketchy and probably not very reliable, but I remember her as a cheerful, rosy-faced body who fitted easily into whatever activity was going on at the time. I do not recall her playing with us – perhaps as a governess she had had enough dealings with children – but she was always friendly and took an interest in the farm and the garden.

In 1943 May and Arthur retired to Parkstone, just outside Bournemouth in Dorset. It was through May, who nursed Louie through her last years, that the letters from Beatrix Potter came into my possession.

When the correspondence with Beatrix begins Louie was forty. She had been governess to Denys Lowson, later to become Sir Denys and Lord Mayor of London. In 1916, however, he had been sent away to school and Louie was looking for a change of occupation. Farming was in her blood. She had been born and brought up on her parents' and grandparents' farm at Harris Bridge, Twycross, Leicestershire, and her Moxon grandparents farmed at Witham-on-the-Hill in Lincolnshire. Beatrix Potter's letter of 15 March 1916 implies that Louie had experience of paid work on a farm. I have been unable to find out where this was. It could not have been at Old Sodbury, since Arthur was away in the trenches and he and May did not buy the farm until after the First World War. All we know is that, having seen the letter in *The Times* (see page 11), Louie wrote to 'A Woman Farmer', offering her services on the farm. Thus began a friendship and correspondence which continued until Beatrix Potter's death in 1943.

Mollie Green (Mollie Byers in one of the letters), now in her nineties and still living in Sawrey, remembers Louie Choyce as something of a character in the village, and very keen on country dancing. This was an interest Louie shared with her employers. Although Beatrix did not dance

THE CHOYCE FAMILY TREE

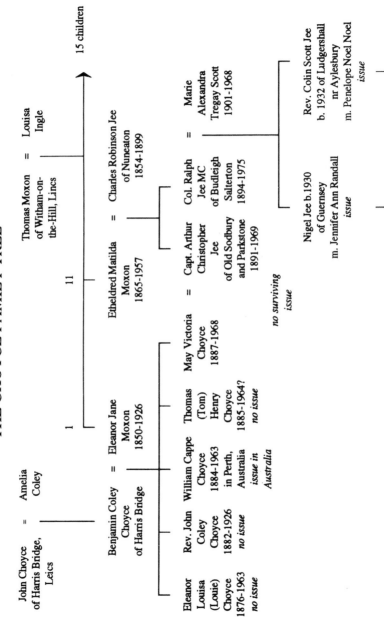

John Choyce
of Harris Bridge,
Leics

=

Amelia
Coley

Thomas Moxon
of Witham-on-
the-Hill, Lincs

=

Louisa
Ingle

→ 15 children

11

1

Benjamin Coley
Choyce
of Harris Bridge

=

Eleanor Jane
Moxon
1850-1926

Etheldred Matilda
Moxon
1865-1957

=

Charles Robinson Jee
of Nuneaton
1854-1899

Eleanor
Louisa
(Louie)
Choyce
1876-1963
no issue

Rev. John
Coley
Choyce
1882-1926
no issue

William Cappe
Choyce
1884-1963
in Perth,
Australia
*issue in
Australia*

Thomas
(Tom)
Henry
Choyce
1885-1964?
no issue

May Victoria
Choyce
1887-1968

=

Capt. Arthur
Christopher
Jee
of Old Sodbury
and Parkstone
1891-1969

*no surviving
issue*

Col. Ralph
Jee MC
of Budleigh
Salterton
1894-1975

=

Marie
Alexandra
Tregay Scott
1901-1968

Nigel Jee b.1930
of Guernsey
m. Jennifer Ann Randall
issue

→

Rev. Colin Scott Jee
b. 1932 of Ludgershall
nr Aylesbury
m. Penelope Noel Noel
issue

→

herself, she sat and watched (and sketched) while her husband and Louie energetically joined in.

Several of the letters refer to Louie's singing and it appears that she had a good voice, or at least she was not shy of using it, and she accompanied herself on the piano. In her will Beatrix Potter left her piano to Louie, but sadly it is no longer in the family. I have been unable to discover whether Louie took it south, or disposed of it locally.

Sometimes on her summer visits to Sawrey, Louie was accompanied by her youngest brother, Tom. Nine years her junior, Tom seems never to have had regular employment. When Louie retired from her job as a governess she and Tom shared a cottage, Tuck Mill, near Swindon.

Another brother referred to in the letters was John. He was a parson and because of his delicate health he was given a curacy in Jersey. He died in 1926 at the early age of forty-four. Louie had one other brother, William, who emigrated to Australia. He died in Perth, leaving descendants there.

I have a dim recollection of being taken as a child to visit Louie and Tom in their remote cottage beside a stream. It must have been wartime for the only detail I can remember with total clarity is Tom in his Home Guard uniform. He was wearing round, steel-rimmed spectacles of a kind which are again becoming fashionable, but to my childish eye they looked incongruous.

Neither Louie nor Tom ever married. As they aged they made increasingly long visits to Parkstone, where May and Arthur were then living. Their last years were spent there, sometimes living with May and Arthur and sometimes in a nursing home nearby. Louie died on 30 December 1963, and Tom soon afterwards.

NIGEL JEE

THE LETTERS

In the year following Beatrix Potter's death, when Margaret Lane was collecting material for her biography *The Tale of Beatrix Potter* (Warne, 1946), William Heelis suggested that Louie Choyce might have preserved some of her correspondence with Beatrix, and that in any case she 'may have interesting recollections of her'.

Margaret Lane visited Louie in Parkstone in September 1944, and found that she had indeed kept a bundle of letters. In her letter thanking Louie after her visit, Margaret Lane wrote, 'Next week I shall be going through your collection of letters again, and making extracts. I hope I shall be able to return them to you before very long, but in the meantime they are very safe.' This suggests that Margaret Lane borrowed all the letters to study, although in her book she only made extensive use of the first, with brief extracts from four others.

In 1990 my wife and I visited the Lake District, taking with us a photocopy of one of the letters, in which Beatrix Potter describes her discovery of an oak court cupboard at a remote farm sale (see page 45). The letter is undated, but from the writing paper used, and from the mention of Louie's ailing mother, who died in 1926, it was probably written in 1925. The pencil sketch in the letter, of a cupboard bearing the date 1667, is undoubtedly of the one which still stands opposite the kitchen range at Hill Top.

The letter aroused a good deal of interest at Hill Top and at the Beatrix Potter Gallery in Hawkshead, where the curator showed us the volume of Beatrix Potter's letters, collected and edited by Judy Taylor, which had been published the previous year. Our next port of call was the National Trust shop, where I bought a copy of this excellent book. It was immediately apparent that Judy Taylor had not been aware of the existence of the Choyce letters, and of their present location. She had included part of the first letter, dated March 15 1916, but had been forced to rely on Margaret Lane's partial (and not entirely accurate) transcription. She had obviously suspected that this might have been the case, for she had added a note: 'The original of this letter is missing. The punctuation here follows that of a previous transcription.'

Ever since inheriting the Choyce letters on May's death in 1968, I had assumed that since Margaret Lane had seen all of them, their contents would be well known to Beatrix Potter scholars. It now dawned on me that if their existence were unknown, nobody could be expected to know that they were now in the Channel Islands. So on returning home I wrote to Judy Taylor to tell her of the collection. I was both surprised and delighted by her enthusiastic response, and a correspondence began which has culminated in this publication.

Short extracts from some of the Choyce letters were included in an article of mine which appeared in *Country Living* in January 1992, and in John Heelis's *The Tale of Mrs William Heelis – Beatrix Potter* (Leading Edge, 1993). The complete collection of letters to Louie Choyce is published here for the first time.

NIGEL JEE May 1994

EDITOR'S NOTE

I remember very clearly the day in November 1990 when there was an envelope from the Channel Islands among our daily clutch of letters. Although I had become quite used to receiving envelopes addressed in an unfamiliar hand, I had a feeling that there was something special about this one, and when I read Nigel Jee's letter telling me about his inherited 'bundle of letters' I knew my instinct had been right. In my excitement, I was much too impatient to wait for a further exchange by post and I reached for the telephone.

Over the next six weeks, kind and generous Nigel Jee copied and despatched all thirty-eight letters to me. I can confess now that my elation on reading them was slightly tinged with disappointment that they had not resurfaced *before* I had completed my years of preparation of *Beatrix Potter's Letters* (Warne, 1989) but, on the other hand, it was the existence of that book that brought them to light again. Now, through the support of The Beatrix Potter Society, they are published, and an important, and much more personal, side of Beatrix Potter's life is revealed.

The letters show how Beatrix's friendship with Louie Choyce deepened over their nearly thirty years of acquaintance, how they shared a love of the piano and of singing, of local gossip and of gardens. However, always aware of the correctness of the style of that period, Beatrix never addressed Louie more intimately than 'My dear Miss Choyce' – though she did progress from 'Yours sincerely, Beatrix Heelis' to 'With much love, yrs aff, Beatrix Heelis' over the years. Occasionally she even referred to Louie as 'Choycey' in letters to others but only once, in 1925, did she go so far to Louie direct.

There is no doubt that Louie Choyce was equally fond of her employer-turned-friend. In a letter to Frederick Warne, written on 14 January 1944 only three weeks after Beatrix Potter's death, she called her, 'My beloved friend . . . What a wonderful woman she was & beloved all over the world.'

Following the style of my previous collections I have annotated these letters wherever I felt it necessary and when I have been able to do so, but this correspondence should be read with both *Beatrix Potter's Letters* and *Letters to Children* (Warne, 1992) close at hand so the exchange can be seen in context with what else was going on in Beatrix's life at the time. I have assumed a certain knowledge on the part of the reader, especially of the intricacies of the Heelis family tree, and as before I have retained Beatrix's punctuation and sometimes eccentric spelling. Beatrix and Louie have not been separately indexed as their shared interests and enthusiasms and details about their lives are interwoven continuously throughout the text.

A number of people have been helpful in the preparation of this publication, particularly Enid Bassom, John Heelis, Anne Hobbs, Nigel Jee, Libby Joy and Willow Taylor. Frederick Warne, the publishers of *Beatrix Potter's Letters* and *Letters to Children*, and Nigel Jee, the owner of the Choyce Letters, have both given their permission for publication. My thanks to them all.

JUDY TAYLOR

ILLUSTRATION ACKNOWLEDGEMENTS

The photographs and illustrations on the pages listed are reproduced by kind permission of the following: 27, John Heelis (from his book *The Tale of Mrs William Heelis – Beatrix Potter*, Leading Edge, 1993); cover (right), frontispiece, 6, Nigel Jee; 65, Museum of Fine Arts, Boston; 33, Private Collection; 36, 42, 48, Victoria & Albert Museum; cover (left), Frederick Warne Archives (photograph from Charles G. Y. King).

THE TIMES *of 7 March 1916 carried a report of the inaugural meeting of the Women's National Land Service, and was followed by an article urging farmers to release men to the war and to employ women in their place – but to pay them adequately.* THE TIMES *of 13 March carried a letter from Beatrix Potter using the pseudonym 'A Woman Farmer'.*

10 March 1916
To the Editor of *The Times*. WOMEN ON THE LAND
Sir, – In your leader upon the employment of women you say that the chief step is the offer of adequate wages. The custom of employing women upon farms has never quite ceased in the north, but the supply of women is undoubtedly affected by the competition of munition work. I pass no opinion as to whether munition workers are extravagantly paid; I only know that farmers cannot compete with their wages. Three girls have gone from adjoining farms here; they expect to earn at least £2 wages per week. They are trained dairymaids and milkers, but totally inexperienced in mechanics. The present waste of skilled training is unfortunate. At one and the same time I was receiving from a Labour Exchange advice to take outside women on my farm; from another Labour Exchange requests for the character of my cowman's daughters for munitions; and my little general servant was being canvassed to go on the land (from which I should presumably have been removed to do the housework). I have worked on it for years and love it; but I still feel some sympathy with the perplexity of the farmers. Harm is being done by the ridiculous and vulgar photographs which appear in the Press. I am perfectly ready to employ the right sort of woman. French women and North country girls have found it possible to work in a short petticoat, and they have not required the theatrical attractions of uniform and armlet to induce them to do their duty.

Yours truly,
A Woman Farmer

To Louie Choyce   Hill Top Farm
                                                       Sawrey
                                                       Ambleside
                                                       March 15. 16

Dear Madam,

Your letter reached me this morning; do you mind telling me are you a girl or middle aged?

I am 50 this year – very active and cheerful; but I am afraid I & my farm housekeeper are both going to be over worked.

I must explain at once that I don't depend on the farm for a living, so some people might not call it real "war work"; but I have farmed my own land for 10 years as a business (before & since marriage) and I have got it into such good order it would be a pity to let it go down.

Probably the farm where you were so useful was *larger* & *better*; they are small about here. This is between Windermere & Coniston; very pretty hilly country but not wild like Keswick or Ullswater. 5 miles station, close to small village, 120 acres, 9 arable the rest meadow hay & hill pastures, 2 horses, 9 or 10 cows, young stock (rear many calves) 60 sheep, 47 being lambing ewes.

My husband is a solicitor; as there are all sorts of people in the world I may say he is a very quiet gentleman, & I am a total abstainer!! We have been 2 years married, no family. We live very quietly in a cottage [Castle Cottage] separate from the old farm house [Hill Top], I have one young servant here. On the farm I have employed a family for 10 years, John Cannon, cowman-foreman-shepherd, Mrs C. dairywoman farm house-keeper. *Willie C.* ploughman horseman. A second son enlisted 1914; when the youngest boy left school & is now 16½, a growing lad.

Willie [C] is reserved [exempted from military service because of his occupation], but we all expect (& rather think he ought) to go, he is finishing the ploughing.

The 2 daughters – very fine strong nice girls – helped their mother on leaving school & then did very well indeed at the C.C dairy school, & took good situations.

The younger has thrown up a place as forewoman in a cheese factory; the elder a good private place. She was home for some months & I told her candidly I thought it would be still more patriotic & much more sensible to take a man's place as cowman.

John seems resigned to "manage somehow". There will be many farmers in worse case. But he is a little man liable to knock up. I really ought not to need his eldest son, if JC were stronger. He & the lad will manage the horse work & sowing down; but I am quite sure his wife & I will be over worked. My husband helps with the hay, but he is short handed too.

I have poultry, orchard, flower garden, vegetables (help with heavy digging no glass), cooking here with the girl's assistance; Mrs C. I & this girl all help with hay, & I single turnips when I can find time, & look after some intake land on the fell.

If I could find a pleasant young lady to help me, this summer, especially with the garden & haymaking it would be a great help. And I often wonder what would happen in the dairy if Mrs Cannon knocked up. If you do not know north country folks you would think them at first reserved & stand offish with strangers; but they are a most decent quiet intelligent family.

It is best to speak straight out; the great difficulty with a stranger woman is the boarding. I can see Mr Heelis does not want a lady living here. I don't think a lady would live comfortably (for either party) in the Cannon's back kitchen.

There remains the front part of the farm house, which I used before I married, & which we still use for spare bedrooms, library etc.

Could I find a young woman who would not feel it too dull to live there *in summer*, & who would not feel hurt or huffy? It is a lovely old house, in fact the furniture & old oak is so good I can only have a careful occupier. There are 2 doors through to the farm quarters, but it is complete in every way (except a fixed bath). There is both fireplace with an oven, & a stove; but the young lady's cooking would have to be managed somehow amongst us, that would be too silly!

I could get her acquainted with two or 3 pleasant families, & there is a tennis club at Hawkshead, 2 miles. I don't go out much, haven't time; & the little town seems nothing but gossip & cards.

I'm afraid our own special sin is not attending church regularly; not loving the nearest parson; & I was brought up a dissenter. There is a good church at Hawkshead, Canon Irving.

I am sorry to trouble you to read such an immense letter (& have missed post); but in writing to a stranger it seems necessary to explain so much.

What do you mean about "hoeing"? I particularly need help in *weeding*, in garden but I use a fork & it is very light drying soil. We both like your letter, it reads so genuine & straight forward; and not many people would have cheerfully tackled that work. Did you receive a salary, or do you mean 'piece work', "according to work etc?" puzzled me? I write to the Times on behalf of the farmers, but I personally can afford to pay proper wages.

I have missed one girl, I answered her advt. too late. I doubt if she had that much work in her; but curiously enough she knew this part & I knew the people she is with in London.

If you like this letter & write again – how can I know more about you? Have you a photograph & a reference to a neighbouring family to ask what manner of girl you are? You mustn't think this rude. I am very downright; but I get on with every body. I can make jam, while there is sugar; but should be glad to learn more cooking! Your letter is very earnest; I wonder if you have a sense of humour!

Yrs sincerely
Beatrix Heelis.

Sawrey,
Ambleside
March 20th 16

Dear Miss Choyce,

Thank you very much for your letters and the addresses. I am writing today to Mrs Hall. I think you seem a *most useful* friend, I only feel a little uncertainty whether so much experience as you have had would not be rather wasted in this post – so we won't decide anything for a few days till I have thought it over and considered Mrs Hall's answer. It is a long way to come if either of us found we had made a mistake!

Your being older than I imagined [Louie Choyce was forty years old] is really an advantage – you look strong, and sensible –

I had not thought of having anyone until *after Easter*.

I remain yrs sincerely
Beatrix Heelis

Square pegs in round holes again! I believe my other correspondent, Miss Drew[?], who wanted to be altogether an outdoor girl (and untrained) – will find she has too hurriedly taken a post as domestic help.

Louie Choyce was duly appointed. She arrived in Sawrey feeling ill and soon afterwards the local doctor diagnosed measles. Beatrix at once wrote to Miss Choyce's previous employer to see if her young charge there, Denys Lowson, might also have been infected, and then she wrote to reassure Louie Choyce's mother.

Sawrey,
Ambleside
Ap. 29.16

Dear Mrs Lowson,

I am very glad to hear your boy is alright. I could only tell you it was measles as the doctor positively said so; but I have maintained all along that it is a sort of influenza with a heat rash. When we were at Appleby at Easter, my brother-in-law, a strong man over 50 had a sharp attack of influenza $104\frac{1}{2}°$ and then rather to their surprise & alarm he came out with a rash all over. I suppose it is some new variety of influenza, nobody suggested *he* had measles!

We told Dr Leadbetter about it, but he said he had never seen a rash with influenza, & as she had been with children, he maintained *they* would be in bed too by this time!

Miss Choyce was feeling her back when she arrived, I noticed her sitting on the hearthrug, and offered her some Elliman [Ellerman's Liniment] – She seemed better next morning, but not much appetite, & in the middle of the afternoon she suddenly seemed very tired & chilly. She had been coughing a little but I'm sure her eyes were not running, like measles. And she said she was afraid she might have got influenza because there was a woman with it in the train. The doctor hasn't been again yet; Nurse Barton says she is going on nicely, she slept fairly well. The rash came out suddenly after hot bread & milk.

It is awkward for you, as you will be wanting to send the boy back to school. And I am in the same doubt about the farm pupil here.

I would prefer influenza, because it comes out quicker! We are not safe about measles for a fortnight; but I really don't believe she has got it.

I remain yrs sincerely
Beatrix Heelis

Sawrey
Ambleside
May 2.16

Dear Mrs Choyce,

What an epidemic! I am glad to say Miss Choyce is going on as well as possible; and now *very good*. I was afraid at first it was going to be a difficult matter to keep her in as she didn't feel ill, and the old woman who is with her has not quite the authority of a hospital nurse. But your letter and her sister's (and doubtless her own commonsense) has impressed on her that [it] is rash to make light of even a mild case of measles, especially while there is an east wind. She is coming downstairs tomorrow, & the doctor says if the hot weather lasts she can go out in the sun on Friday in the farm garden.

It was a most unlucky beginning. But I am glad it did not break out the very next day, as I had time to get a little acquainted, and I saw that she was going to be a very helpful worker.

There is a great deal of infectious illness this year, the measles were bad all winter, & now I hear of another case as well as your daughter's; and influenza is about too – In spite of having rather offended the doctor by the suggestion – I can't help thinking her symptoms were rather like 'flue', she complained of her back – not of a cold – and Mr Heelis's eldest brother at Appleby was struck in the same way, like your son. I suppose it is another of the many side troubles from this terrible war; I am glad it is nothing worse in Miss Choyce's case.

I think she will soon be able to do a little, when I was talking to her through the window she was darning stockings & very merry.

Really the most awkward part of it is the doubt about infection, both for Mrs Lowson & ourselves. But nobody could foresee or help it!

With kind regards

Yrs sincerely
Beatrix Heelis

In THE TALE OF BEATRIX POTTER *Margaret Lane quotes extracts from a letter (now lost) in which Louie Choyce tells her mother of her first impressions of her employers:* 'Mrs Heelis I like very much. She is quite out of the common . . . short, blue-eyed, fresh-coloured face, frizzy hair brushed tightly back, dresses in a tweed skirt pinned at the back with a safety pin . . . Mr Heelis is a quiet man, very kind. They believe together in a simple life.'
   On 25 May, Louie wrote to her mother again:

It is so lovely here now the lilacs are out & there are such quantities & the azaelaes [sic] are wonderful. I have never seen so many & so fine, it is perfectly beautiful. We are busy gathering broom tips, sphagnum moss, & planting heaps of lavendar [sic] plants for next year, everything in Eeswyke is going on well, we have to walk a mile or two to get the Broom & then we get Foxglove leaves and Barberry. There are 4 monster bushes of Honeysuckle azaela [sic] in Eeswyke & every other I know of . . .
   I get up early but Mrs Heelis isn't a bit of a driver. She finds me odd jobs if it is too hot or wet to garden & never fusses. I simply do like her exceedingly . . .
   With much love tell John [her brother, four years younger and a parson] I wish he was here but as we are all so busy we couldn't entertain him only 'tis so lovely he couldn't help liking it. The Mr Heelis [Willie's brother, Arthur John] a parson helps in the hay himself.

The mention of Eeswyke is puzzling but it would appear that Beatrix and Louie were looking after the garden there, too.
   At one time it was thought that Louie brought her brother, Tom, with her and stayed until the end of the war in 1918 but it now appears that her first visit was probably a short one and that she was by herself. In October 1916 Beatrix sent one of her books to Louie's old pupil, Denys Lowson. His thank you letter came to her as 'a pleasing surprise. I perceive that "Choicey" has taught you to write a good round hand; and to be a polite little gentleman . . . She will have a great deal to tell you about Tom kittens [sic] house, and all our rabbits, and potatoes, & cats, & cows. I think you ought to come and see them some day *when she is here again.' [My emphasis.]*
   And in a letter to Millie Warne on 15 December 1916 Beatrix wrote, 'Labour is a great anxiety . . . I had a woman (lady) help last summer who is coming back, we expect rather a strenuous summer.'

*There is no mention of Louie Choyce in any of Beatrix's letters that we have
after that date until the next letter that has survived, written to Louie on 13 May
1921, but from the tone of the ensuing letters I would surmise that Louie had been
a regular summer visitor and helper. The intervening years were certainly busy
ones for Beatrix. She told Millie in that same December 1916 letter, 'I hardly
know what "legs" are, & seldom sit down except to meals.' The ploughman was
finally called up by the army early in 1917, and weeks of rain later in the year
delayed first the haymaking and then the grain harvest.*

*As well as managing the farms, Beatrix was also in continuous touch with
Frederick Warne.* THE STORY OF MISS MOPPET *and* THE STORY OF A
FIERCE BAD RABBIT *were both reissued in the* PETER RABBIT *Series in October
1916 and* TOM KITTEN'S PAINTING BOOK *was published in June 1917. For
all three Beatrix provided pictures for the cover but she could only find the time to
draw after supper, 'with eyes that . . . are beginning to feel anno domini'. To help
Warne out of serious financial trouble in 1917, she looked out the manuscript of
an illustrated book of rhymes she had first offered to them in 1905,* APPLEY
DAPPLY'S NURSERY RHYMES, *and an abridged edition was published in
October that year. The merchandise featuring characters from the little books
was encouraged, with handkerchiefs, stationery and china all appearing on the
market. Beatrix also worked on* THE TALE OF JOHNNY TOWN-MOUSE *during
much of 1918 and, although she only delivered the last of the pictures at the end of
August, it was published that December.*

*The reconstructed firm of Frederick Warne & Company Limited was regis-
tered on 25 May 1919 and Fruing Warne was appointed Managing Director.
Beatrix had agreed that her considerable overdue royalties would be paid to her
mainly in the form of debentures and shares. She was constantly being asked for a
new book and even made a start but found that she just couldn't do it. 'My eyes
are always tired.'*

Sawrey
Ambleside
May 13.21

My dear Miss Choyce

I have kept intending to write to you; sundry worries but no illness! and now there has been warm thunder rain, which is a relief on the farm, as we were either over stocked with a big crop of lambs, or else very backward with grass. It seemed as though it would never come. It is not long since we had deep snow one morning! Things are more backward here; but still the lilac & azaleas and apple blossom are coming out; and I hope our singing bird will arrive before they are over – railway strikes permitting. I do not think a railway strike would last; a great many are unwilling to go out, and I think the colliers will dribble back. A general strike now, with the union funds exhausted, would be very much less serious than it would have been at the beginning. The worst side of it is the complete indifference to the damage done to the country and trade. I should think Lincoln is not a very accessable [sic] place, I wonder how Mrs Fowkes gets backward & forward, I could ask her; I think you would easily get here from Birmingham, either by Crewe, onto the LNW to Windermere; or by Leeds & the Middland [sic] to Carnforth and Lakeside (or Ulverston) if local branch did not fit. I do hope your visit won't fall through, and provided Mrs Lowson has not booked you again for the holidays, I should be so very glad if you could stay on here, at any salary you name; it seems to me if May [Louie's youngest sister] is not quite strong and your mother sometimes wanting you, it might suit everybody better than your taking another permanent post at once. Though for that matter, it is reported that both the local public houses are likely to be vacant!! There's your chance! It is a deplorable season, the hotels are empty; and without coal.

My mother keeps well, her illness has perhaps aged her a bit. But she is again able to drive up here [from her home in Windermere] . . .

[The end of this letter is missing.]

Willie Heelis was the youngest of eleven children, four girls and seven boys. Some time in the summer of 1922 it was decided that his bachelor brother, Arthur John, the Rector of Brougham, was too ill to continue his incumbency or to stay any longer by himself in the large rectory, and Beatrix agreed that he should come to stay at Castle Cottage. George and Grace Heelis, mentioned in the next letter, were two of Willie's other siblings.

Sawrey
Ambleside
Sept 19.22

My dear Miss Choyce,

I am owing you two letters – but really I have never had time or (what shall I say?) equanimity to write to a cheerful body! This season has been a nightmare, I shall always look back to it with a memory of rushing up cocks, & rushing in loads of corn in a gale of wind with small rain coming in from the sea and ending in a pelt. We have only had one fine spell, Monday Sept 4th to Sept 11th since you left. Four days of it were hot, and we got in 2 fields of hay and the ley corn without a drop of rain. And John Taylor & I rushed some of the remaining corn into a little stack under a cart sheet. [John Taylor, who lived in the cottage in Post Office Lane, was John Joiner in *The Tale of Samuel Whiskers*.] We have only a cart or two of hay still out, we got the clover corn yesterday under very nervous conditions, ending in a downpour which is still continuing. We were a fortnight in the post office meadow; except during the dry week we have had to cut little bits, and work it over & over. But we have had very little damaged by dint of hard work. Four carts of clover were very bad; they had been in cock a month. I salted the mow, I expect it will eat with the oats, which are excellent. All crops are a bit short. I shall have to sell some cattle. Was it after you left, the heifer hanged herself at Hawkshead Field? fell over a bank with its hind foot in a rabbit hole under a tree root. I have a nice family of little pigs arrived last Wednesday night (torrents of rain). As a rule the nights have been clear and cold; I think the extreme coldness of the earth has caused our bad weather, it has often been fine at Kendal, when we were in sea fog. On top of the hay making the Revd [Arthur John Heelis] has had several illnesses, and there have been holiday visitors, first George Heelis & Colin & Rosemary [George's children], and then Esther & Nancy and their eldest brother Richard Nicholson [Grace Heelis's children]. Nancy & Esther both very happy at schools & doing well. They asked after you! He [Richard] is a fine fellow and a *terrible* fisher man, he is going to British Columbia, seems to have an opening & know a little already of fruit growing. He had some outlandish Canadian lake flies; and he & Uncle Willie by moonlight caught – or poached – trout in such numbers up at the tarn that I rebelled. They were red, like salmon, and made me think of the revolt of the London apprentices in the middle ages against a salmon diet. We daren't give them away & it was no weather for posting fish, so they put back quantities. The biggest weighed lbs3. I don't suppose he would have continued to catch, the fish happened to be on the feed, and were near spawning. I never saw such ugly black monsters. I think they must feed on tadpoles in the mud. The village people don't know there are fish in the tarn, & it is not advisable to enlighten them. The young people were very merry and their visits were a success in spite of the weather. I had Mary back to get supper & wash up as I could not manage. By the way, she informed one of them that this rain is a judgement upon the wickedness of the world. It seems curious it should fall upon herself & her cousin Hannah, who consider themselves saved? Mrs Rogerson [Beatrix's housekeeper] has made your arrowroot pudding successfully, also steamed puddings. – and "custards", I wished I could have checked the latter, while the hens were moulting, her custard is like very fluid buttered egg! The hens are beginning to lay alright again, no pullet eggs yet they were hatched rather late. The 9 big turkey chicks are fine birds; there were a lot of nests hatched out in July, turkey chickens all over the place but all have died except 5 – over 30 – Last summer I did not lose one of the late hatched. The cold & damp have not done well for the poor Revd A.J. He seemed to get a chill about end of July and was in bed a week, attended by Dr Brownlie from Windermere and Nurse. He was very uncomplaining and patient. He has altered a good deal since you were here. In a sense he is better; much more normal, not so red faced and flabby; and we hear less about his "mind"; but he sits indoors reading or playing chess by himself and he is thinner. I hope if it would only come warm he would get about more, he had got to shooting rabbits, & going to Hawkshead to the reading room before he took worse. His troubles seem to be digestive & kidney, complicated by some displacement from a bad operation for appendicitis 9 years ago. Nurse thought he was very ill the first night. It does not seem to matter much. I hope – in a depressed way – he is more resigned. He will just have to make the best of small comforts. He has a fancy to go to Silloth later on, where he is known at the hotel and looked after; then he will have to go back to his sisters at Appleby for a bit; but I fancy he will be glad to come back here in spring. I don't want to keep him over the winter; for one thing he needs a fire, there is hardly room in that bedroom. Also no inside W.C. His furniture sale made about £600. He had better have gone into that trade – a set of 7 chairs which had cost some price between £5 and £10 made £54, and a mahogany wardrobe jumped from £8 to £40. Some things were thrown away, and some were sold which he had wished to keep. I was not sufficiently acquainted with the things; & I make mistakes at sales. I bought some things, including 3 chairs rather like those at the farm.

Now this is all about our concerns! I am so glad you had a good time at the Lowsons, you don't mention Selby in your last. Have you really chucked it!? or have you been persuaded to go back? [Louie had been working at Turnham Hall, Selby, and must have returned, as she addressed a letter from there dated 'Xmas 1922'] I did not think you would want to stay another winter. What shall I do with the grey coat & skirt I had them cleaned & the skirt unpicked. There is a great quantity of fruit, small & unripe & much falling off. I shall now turn my mind upon apple & blackberry jelly. I hope you find your mother pretty well. I am interested to hear of your sister's plans. They will have no difficulty in selling a small farm.

Yrs aff.

Beatrix Heelis

My mother keeps very well, & the telephone is on, but alas she cannot hear it, a disappointment. But it is a great convenience to be able to speak to the house keeper.

Sawrey

Nr Ambleside

Dec 13th. 22

My dear Miss Choyce,

It is always cheering to hear from you – even if you are in a dull and dismal climate – you are quite chirpy in your grumbles! The thrushes are singing here. We have two dark wet days, which we do not like after the fine weather, it has been a wonderful autumn.

Some people still have their young cattle out; ours have been in at night this last fortnight. It has spared the hay. There is beginning to be a great deal of (mild) influenza, I hope I may keep clear over the Annual Nursing meeting next week, as the Secretary is ill; and I hope this Christmas I have the gratification of sorting out my turkeys, there are not enough to go round the customers – I lost such a lot of the July hatched. [In 1919 Beatrix had helped to set up a Nursing Association for the three villages of Hawkshead, Sawrey and Wray. She was Honorary Treasurer.]

Your hens have done remarkably well, eggs have been very scarce; and saleable at 4/6 per dozen if anybody had had any to sell. My pullets have looked like laying for a month past, but they won't start, though I have been giving them meat offal.

What a sad loss for Mrs Alkin, he would be one of the children in that pretty photograph. I remember you telling me what a sad long failing Mr Alkin had had. I noticed the article on Purcell, I will look it up again, we have the paper.

It is sad about your brother being ill away in Jersey, it is well that you know he is with kind people, but it must be a worry.

Here – I am contending with the Revd, a curious situation – he is reinforced by my own good nature. I admit that it seems a shame to root him out, especially in bad weather! While it was fine we let him drift on, as it seemed better for him to be in the country. But it is *not* reasonable to keep him the year round. He had a wish to go to Blackpool, but the hydro is full over Xmas, when I particularly want to be free; I think Wm. will run him over to his sisters at Appleby on the Saturday before Xmas, and afterwards he will go to Blackpool and then come back here. He is *very* much better; he always will be eccentric, and rather helpless. I don't dislike the prospect of his spending a good deal of his remaining days here (which he obstinately places at 2 yrs 6 weeks!!) [Arthur John lived for another three years] but it is rather awkward in winter. I think it really needs another bedroom, and what house agents call "indoor sanitation" to be comfortable. His "mind" has so far recovered as to admit holding political set to's with "Possy" [Mr Postlethwaite] in the smithy and usually getting the best of it. He was very unwilling to go back Appleby direction; possibly rather shy after making such muddles of his affairs, which was not all together excusable by bad health. His two elderly sisters came over one day last summer from Appleby and he bolted to Hawkshead, and stopped out till 8 o'clock! His preference for our society is touching; but excessive!

I consider I was defrauded of the piano & folk songs last time, and just when you were in particularly good voice. I wonder how long he will stay away; whether you could have paid a visit here before going south again, we must see later on.

Mrs Rogerson has been away with a chill, but she is alright again. The Mackereths are all well, I haven't heard just lately from Mrs Cannon, no doubt I will do so at Christmas when I send her a couple of rabbits. The men are trapping such fat ones. [John Mackereth had replaced John Cannon as farm manager at Hill Top.]

If you please I am a *butcher*! We have been butching on the quiet for a long time, and someone reported (one of the professional butchers as a matter of fact). He did nobody any harm but himself. We had always been careful to kill in the open air. The Council have now licensed the hall next the washhouse at Hill Top. We find that a sheep or lamb home killed makes about 20/- more than market price and we can sell good meat for less than the butcher after all. Which the Council approve of; for once showing a little common sense.

I wonder what the roads will be like in a few years, the motor traffic last summer between Windermere & Ambleside was 120 per cent increased from the summer before. There is no unemployment about here, but I am afraid things are very bad at Barrow. And I doubt if any govt. can do very much to improve matters; trade will gradually have to find its level.

This little book [*Cecily Parsley*] has just come out, they are nearly all very old drawings. You will recognize the bluebell wood, up Stones [Stoney] Lane behind this house.

My mother keeps well. She is not coming today as it is wet & windy; it is a great comfort to have the telephone at the post office. It would be a joke to ring you up some day, but I think we would have to make appointment by letter. I find trunk calls even to Kendal involve long waits at the post office. With much love and good wishes for Christmas

yrs aff
Beatrix Heelis

Pity there was not room for the "red rose" verse. The other two verses fit beautifully. I have written your name in one copy & "autographed" the others.

Since the publication of THE TALE OF JOHNNY TOWN-MOUSE *in December 1918 Warne had been urging Beatrix to do a new book but, although she started work on* 'The Tale of The Birds and Mr Tod' *the following year, it did not find favour and was finally abandoned. It was the visit to Castle Cottage in June 1921 of Anne Carroll Moore, Superintendent of Children's Work at the New York Public Library, that at last brought about the publication of a new book. Beatrix had shown Miss Moore her portfolios of drawings, among them those for a collection of nursery rhymes begun thirty years before. She had suggested in 1917 that Warne might publish them as a sequel to* APPLEY DAPPLY'S NURSERY RHYMES *but they had rejected the idea, hoping that Beatrix would write another story. Miss Moore's enthusiasm encouraged Warne to ask to see the rhymes again and Beatrix agreed to rework some of the drawings so that* CECILY PARSLEY'S NURSERY RHYMES *could be published for Christmas 1922.*

In THE HISTORY OF THE WRITINGS OF BEATRIX POTTER *Leslie Linder states that Beatrix's guinea pig watercolour inscribed 'H. B. P. Jan. '93' was done specifically for the rhyme that starts, 'We have a little garden'. However, for Christmas 1922, Louie Choyce sent a copy of* CECILY PARSLEY'S NURSERY RHYMES *to her old pupil, Denys Lowson, accompanied by the following:*

I am sending you ... this of Mrs Heelis to put amongst your others as the little rhyme of the garden is mine, only she hadn't room for the middle verse which is:–

> "Sweet mignonette & larkspur
> Blue Lupin & Sweet Peas
> White Rocket & Escholtzia [sic]
> I've some of each of these"
>
> And in the very middle
> A Fair white lily grows
> And by its side contrasting well
> A beautiful red rose"'

Louie Choyce's letter ended, 'You see at a glance in Cecily Parsley Mrs H is not a Prohibitionist, a nice slap for her American friends.' This is a reference to Cecily Parsley's brewing of 'good ale' or, in the picture, of cowslip wine. In the original illustration Beatrix had shown Cecily brewing cider from red apples and had been asked to make the change by Warne, who were obviously unaware of the alcoholic content of cowslip wine.

In the next letter Beatrix is referring to an ancient May Day custom. THE TIMES
*of 1 May 1923 reproduced two prints of May Day celebrations a hundred years
before, one of them 'a dance round a ''Jack-in-the-Green'',' a circular frame-
work covered in leaves concealing a man or a boy.*

Sawrey

May 2. 23

My dear Miss Choyce

Were we not talking about Jack-in-the-greens? I cut this out of the
Times; my recollection of them in Kensington in the seventies is like this,
only the milkmaids were more in the Dolly Varden style, with straw hats,
aprons, & ribbons.

I forgot to give you news of Fenella when I wrote; she clucked but she
did not sit! I think she is laying again. I brought her over here when the Hill
Top garden was planted with potatoes, so she is promenading with that
Campine Cockerel, I fancy they agree better, the hens treat her with
respect.

We are having a sad time with the poor Revd. He insisted in coming
back in cold weather, & for a week he crept about the village, looking very
thin, but with a promising appetite. Then he got an influenza cold which
brought back his bladder troubles. I managed for a fortnight with Nurse
Filkin's help, then he was worse last Sunday, & we got a nurse from
Ulverston. It is very touching that he should be so anxious to come back;
but there is no hope of his ever being anything but an invalide [sic]; & quite
impossible to predict. His heart is weak & he might go suddenly; but
myself I think he will last some time, wearing out by repeated illnesses. He
is too ill to move at present, & it could only be to a nursing home if he went.
It is rather a puzzle.

The fruit damsons seem set, plums doubtful, apples not out, & not
much budding. The daffodils have been most lovely, the garden is very
pretty, tulips coming on.

I shall send this by Portishead, unless I can find your letter with the
address. I am so very glad you have found a post with people you know
something about. I hope you left your mother pretty well. My mother is
coming round by Ambleside this afternoon, the ferry boat is off for spring
cleaning. She will have a pleasant drive, it is a lovely spring day, very warm
& sunny. We have a small crop of lambs, mostly big strong singles. I have a
hatch of 9 chickens, every body complains of small lafters[?]. I have just

put 20 hen eggs under a turkey; determined to get a crop! Eggs have been 10d to 1/- for a long time, there is no use keeping old hens.

I got a copy of Burne Jones [sic] 22/ in a sale, could have wished it cleaner, but it has Mr Coley's portrait alright, I think you show a strong likeness [Louie's father, Benjamin Coley Choyce, was a cousin of the painter, Sir Edward Coley Burne-Jones, and her grandmother's name was Amelia Coley].

I remain yrs aff.
Beatrix Heelis

Just had a call from Rd McNally to inquire after A.J.H. *most* polite, & agreeable, & me with a conscience that I have not contributed to the augmentation of stipend funds. Whatever is to be done! I will tell WH he must subscribe, in moderation.

The Rev. Arthur John Heelis

Sawrey
July 12th 23

My dear Miss Choyce

Exuse [sic] pencil as I am stirring green gooseberries, there is a good crop of all berries – strawberries unusually good, but there will be no plums or apples to speak of. The weather is suddenly hot, broiling; very fine for hay making, apart from thunder showers & fogs. We have over 40 carts but not half through. Mary has gone for her holiday; everybody has been vaccinated, in consequence of a visitor arriving in Windermere with smallpox; the Rev is intirely [sic] upstairs – and it is pretty hard work! I have an old person, Mattie Coward, from Far Sawrey in the evenings which is a help. I was really afraid to go far from the house, he is so unsafe with matches. I do not know what I would have done without Nurse. (Cast thy bread upon the waters!) I shall pay so much a week to the [Nursing] Association, but it is infinitely less trouble & cheaper than a nurse in the house. I am not having the Nicholsons this holidays, only George Heelis & Colin. Esther is doing well & much liked at Leyburn, & Nancy is happy at school, none too strong – growing, & glands last winter. My Mother is wonderfully well; greatly interested in the vaccination, she herself has not been done yet. I had a genteel small "take" – Mr Heelis's is rubbish – Harry Byers has the worst arm so far. I have a good brood of turkeys. I sold a second brood, & chickens have done very well. I cannot give Fenella a good summer character, I don't think she has laid 10 eggs since you left, continually clucking without sitting – at last I got her on to two eggs near hatching, but she has not much idea – Probably she will lay well in winter after the summer's run. The garden is very full of flowers, the roses are out. It is interesting to hear of Minehead, we spent several Easters there as children. But I confuse it with Ilfracombe – I well remember Dunster & the drives towards Exmoor.

With much love yrs aff
Beatrix Heelis

'The Dutch people' referred to by Beatrix in the next letter were Queen Wilhelmina of the Netherlands, her Consort Prince Henry and their daughter, Juliana, who had been on a five-week private visit to the country, spending three weeks in the Lake District in July.

I cannot trace the reference to Peltze. The matter much in the news at the time was the question of reparations for the war from Germany and the continued occupation by the Allies, and particularly the French, of the Ruhr, where there was considerable passive resistance.

Sawrey
Nr Ambleside
Aug. 21. 23

My dear Miss Choyce,

What comical drawings! they show courage and considerable motion; it is impossible to predict whether any child will develope [sic] artistic talent; they have much more imagination than grown ups; and they can often draw. Sir E.B.J. [Edward Burne-Jones] seems to have made the same observation. What a delightful book it is, I have just finished reading it again. Our hay is *not* in, we are in the last field. August has been atrocious, I do not believe there has been a day (perhaps 3 to be exact, at long intervals) without rain. This last week end has poured in torrents. The corn is getting over ripe, & devoured by sparrows etc. The early part of the haymaking was very successful, it is a very big crop. Colin & his father are coming next week. The girl guides have been in camp, very clampy & merry; they went home yesterday. The Rvd. is a little better; he won't dress or admit any improvement, but we occasionally hear his walking stick, clump clump along the passage upstairs, so he *can* walk. It is rather weird. The summer has not helped him. We had about 4 days oppressively hot, that was all. The Dutch people, by report, were kindly homely folk, great feeders; put up the price of old hens! for soup. The p. consort was disliked as a German, he was affable in shops & went much on the lake. The Queen sketched, & sprained her ankle & was affable to the alarmed Dr Mitchell of Ambleside; & the little princess was never heard of, so there is hope she is being brought up retired; they ordered an iron bedstead for her instead of the old fashioned wooden one. They have now departed. But the trippers have not: The roads are horrible; many accidents. I do not like the aspect of Peltze since the late Entente crisis. I have run against her twice, a smirking fawning doubtfully smiling mixture. I have seen a spaniel look

29

like that, conscious of wrong doing, but not without hope that it may be going to bamboozle its owner & obtain forgiveness. One feels complete confidence in Mr Baldwin; I always did think the French were making a bad mistake, they cannot overcome obstinate passive resistence [sic]. Do you know anything about 3 large keys **⌐** in a dressing table drawer at

Hill Top? I think some visitor must have left them. They are too big for furniture, & they do not belong to any of the room doors there, or here. They look like door keys. Sun coming out between showers. I must stop.

With love yrs aff

H B Heelis – Oh dear how I would like a song

On 12 December 1923 Beatrix wrote to Denys Lowson's mother in London recommending to her a play that had been made of THE TAILOR OF GLOU-CESTER *by Harcourt Williams. 'I think it should be a charming little play; my only doubt is about the* mice. *Even if played by children they would be so over large that they would stultify the point of the tale; little mice and tiny stitches. If I were producing a village performance I would certainly use marionettes, on wires, for the mice – with our "Choycey bird" concealed under the Tailor's table, to provide the mousey singing!*

'I hear from her frequently, I should think her present charges, are rather a handful; spoilt children. . .'

THE TAILOR OF GLOUCESTER *play was published by Warne in 1930.*

Sawrey
Nr Ambleside
March 1. 24

My dear Miss Choyce,

I'm afraid I have been a long time in answering your letter; yes it will suit us quite well – Easter and Whitsuntide are both late – I hope we may get away for a week at Easter, and it might be decent weather. March has come in – like a polar bear! so it may go out as a lamb. The snow is not much but the wind is bitter. The week before was really fine, quite warm in the sun. I was doing a bit of gardening at Hill Top and it was almost hot under the wall. I have some lively chickens, but only 6 of them. The hens are laying well. A.J.H. is still here, there was talk of moving him north but it was much too cold; and very well he did not start as he began a violent cold the day after he should have moved. If he isn't gone by Easter I will send him to the nursing home at Windermere for a fortnight (at someone else's charges.) I do not like to see him ill used when it comes to chucking him out; but he is a tie. Have I written since the Grasmere play. I enjoyed it very much, though it was not so good a play as some others – and the children's part was disappointing. There were 5 of them, excellent; so natural and unaffected; but their singing was only a snatch; and the little girl who had a good deal to say, describing what she had been doing in school – I could not see anything amusing about it, or relevant to the story. Still it was enjoyable, and the hall was packed. It was a dreadfully wet day, & we had a puncture, luckily just getting into Grasmere.

There was a bad motor accident last week. The drunken son in law of old Rev. McNally coming back from Ulverston meddled with the driving wheel; & the hired car, with driver, Harper, & a tipsy friend went head over heels into a field. Harper was killed on the spot. It has nearly finished poor old MacNally [sic] with the shock. I cannot help thinking it is a blessing. The fellow had come into some money upon his mother's death, and was intending to buy a car for hiring out; he was a great danger on the roads when he used to drive for Goodwin. There is very little traffic at present on the roads.

I had the honour of receiving a letter from Mrs Stanley Baldwin the other day, with reference to a charity, the Invalid Children's Aid Association; I had heard from them before through Sir Alfred Fripp the surgeon. They have some scheme for collecting pennies from better-off children by a system of stamped cards, my publishers have been able to accomodate [sic] them with a few thousand little coloured prints which were printed off

31

for the binding of the defunct 1/6 edition. I think these are to be used like coupons on grocery, but I am not quite clear how. I pointed out to Mrs Baldwin that my name has acquired a drawback! we are getting rather annoyed about Mrs Sidney Webb [there was repeated confusion in the newspapers between Beatrix Potter Heelis and Beatrice Potter Webb]. The papers print the untruth prominently, and the contradiction so unprominently that it has no effect to stop the lie. The most laughable part of it was a photograph of Beatrix Potter & her husband – a horrid little fat man with a billy goat beard! Wm. was furious, said it was a libel on *him*.

Denys sent me such a pretty Christmas card, an old Cotswold cottage it looked like. Sorry for the little girls disappointment, but it *was* a long way to bring them. With love & looking forward to your visit & some dear tunes,

yrs aff
Beatrix Heelis.

PS   I can't understand those £300 houses? If Captain Jee can do it with quarried stone it is a remarkable acheivement [sic]. There has been a great discussion at Kendal about houses at that price; some of the town council have been to Belgium and brought back plans for doing it with concrete slabs. If standardized and made in large quantities, (like the American Ford cars) there would be great saving; and one can only hope the houses would not be very hideous.

Captain Arthur Jee was the husband of Louie's sister, May, and had been commissioned in 1913 in the Oxford & Bucks Light Infantry. He owned a quarry in Chipping Sodbury, near their farm in Old Sodbury, and Beatrix's comment implies that he was building houses with his own stone as a speculative venture.

I wonder if you will manage the journey in one day, it will be useless looking at timetables until after Easter; there are more trains later. We will expect you May 25th.

Mr Kipling must have good eyesight if he did a tiny book. I am sure I could not have done the pictures so I am glad I was not asked to! I know someone who contributed two little ornaments.

In 1920 work had begun on the making of a doll's house to be presented to Queen Mary. Under the direction and design of Sir Edwin Lutyens, everything was made as perfectly as possible by selected craftsmen working to scale – one inch to the foot. The walls were hung with seven hundred watercolours painted by living artists and the library contained two hundred books, each one written in the author's own hand and bearing a bookplate designed by E. H. Shepard. Together with Thomas Hardy, Arnold Bennett, Max Beerbohm, Walter de la Mare and Somerset Maugham (among others), an approach was made to Kipling. Verses by Rudyard Kipling was his own choice and included 'If', 'The Road through the Woods', 'The Fairies' Seige' and 'A Charm Recessional', and he decorated some of the poems. Queen Mary's Doll's House is on display in Windsor Castle.

I'm afraid the foot & mouth [contagious cattle disease] order is coming on again, cases between Ulverston & Lancaster, horrid nuisance. I want to sell three calving cows this spring. It is most awkward being unable to get rid of stock.

I doubt if we could get up a play in a fortnight, especially with the present undrilled assortment; you needn't be afraid of *my* doing it *without you*!

Willie Heelis

In April 1924 Beatrix and Willie went to London for a week to clear the old Potter family house, 2 Bolton Gardens, in preparation for putting it on the market. Beatrix wrote years later to an American friend, 'There were the accumulations of 60 odd years – perplexing, overwhelming, grimy with London soot. I had no sentimental repinings as I had been discontented and never strong as a young person in London – but what a task!'

Sawrey,
Nr Ambleside
April 26. 24

My dear Miss Choyce,

You will wonder how we got on in London. It was all work & no play I can assure you! 7.a.m. till 12 p.m. and a scramble to the end. I did *not* buy a hat; and returned rather more ragged than I went. I did one afternoon out, to St Paul's & to see my old Aunt [Mary (Polly) Potter Wrigley, b.1837] on Sunday. She remembered me, by snatches, & forgot again. It was rather touching, she called out "She's calling *me Polly*! Who is she?" When a person survives to be great grand mother, there are not many left to call her by her Christian name. I did do a certain amount of shopping. I bought a carpet and a guinea pig, both extortionate in price. We got back on Thursday before Easter & the goods arrived at Lindeth How [her mother's house in Windermere] on Tuesday – another 3 days of unpacking – wonderfully packed & most obliging men, all done by Harrods, lorry ordered from station etc. The only drawback is that my mother has not been so well as usual; I should have said slight influenza; but the doctor called it a slight chill and bilious ness which has affected her appetite and pulled her down. He says she will pick up when she can get out. There has been pleasant rain here for 24 hours and it is milder, so I hope the weather is changing.

I do not think the arrival of her furniture was very good for her, though she sat in one room and watched through the window, it was a bit tiring and exciting. She has had some poor ugly things put in the drawing room & displaced others; however, it is naturel [sic] to like things she has always used. She did not wish to have the piano, it sold for £90. I don't think she will be in a hurry to sort her drawers & cupboard. Oh dear! the soot! and the moths, in such as were looked. The carpets and get-at-able woolens had been well looked after. A.J.H has returned from the Windermere nursing home; he gained 7lbs in weight, is clothed & quite a reformed character! There is just one drawback; I have always thought he was less in the way upstairs. There is heavy rain & warmer, very welcome.

Yrs aff
Beatrix Heelis

Sawrey
May 12.24

My dear Miss Choyce

Tuesday 27th will do first rate; and as Tuesday is an Ambleside day it probable that Mr Heelis would come back by Windermere and pick you up. There is just one thing troubling me when you speak of the piano, this awful old A.J.H.! I had thoughts of taking it to Hill Top, but then he could scarcely be left alone in the house in the evenings, I believe the best plan will be to get it hoisted upstairs into the big room. He is a complete damper poor man. Sits in the dining room, with a rug, smoking a dirty clay pipe. He is not quite so well again just now, he suddenly began to go out, while he was at the nursing home; and he continued to do so in rain & sleet & carpet slippers, I could have slapped him! He may be away; but it is doubtful.

You needn't be afraid the lilac will be over, it is only black buds still. The pear & damson are nearly full out. We have been having "black thorn winter". I never remember sloe thorns so late, and bitterly cold. Today is really "growy". The poor cattle have suffered; they were turned out in the fine Easter week, the young cattle that is to say; the milk cows are still lying in. Our hay is about finished and there is only very short grass, but it will come with a rush, after the soaking. The daffdls are very pretty. I do hope your brother Tom gets that post, what a good thing it would be. I've had another letter about plays, oddly enough. I think I will send you this Nutkin to ask Miss Joan's opinion! You see it turns altogether on singing games, for padding out and prettyness. My idea (as regards printing) would be to make little 6d or 4d booklets with explanations and two or three outline sketches. I would like to do one with little Lucy [sic] of Newlands as leading lady, and work in rather more adventures than come into the Tiggy book.

And a third more of a sort of 'ballet' version of Peter Rabbit in which a batch of little cabbage-girls should do a sort of morris dance.

I still have ideas in my old head; but neither spare time nor perseverance.

I am about sick of that furniture – what with my mother asking for things I never saw, and various disappointments, it seems like a variation of the prayer book. 'I have brought the things I ought not to have done, & left the things that etc.'

It will be very refreshing to see you again. I think we will get that piano upstairs. The room is much improved. I have been using it more lately. The chickens have suffered from the weather. I have one to hen [?] hatched; and another sitting on the eggs which she is eating by degrees. I must go out & fight them away from her. I am sending you £2 towards expenses.

Yrs aff

H.B. Heelis

Sawrey
June 17.24

My dear Miss Choyce,

I was so glad to get your letter, and very interested about the houses. I should think Capt. Jee has got some men who *work*. They sound from your description to be very nice commodious dwellings. It seems that even in a stone country he finds it best to use concrete. It does seem rediculous [sic] to plunge the country into a further enormous debt to bolster up bricklaying.

The weather has played you a very nasty unkind trick! Friday Saturday were glorious hot days, Sunday cold & drizzle, now today, Tuesday, is a hot windy day again, we shall soon be hay making if this intends to last. Yesterday evening was the first really warm night. Mr Heelis & I fished (at least I rowed!) till darkness; coming down the lane about 11. It was lovely on the tarn, not a breath of wind & no midges. The fish were "taking short", running at the fly without getting hooked, but he caught 4 which was plenty. We put back the smallest, the other 3 weighed over 4 lbs together, the biggest was 1lb 10oz. They were exciting to catch as they fought & made rushes to get under the boat. I see the first rose is coming out at Hill Top. J B. & I had a day's tidying there. Now I have ducklings on my conscience, & must stop. Possy's have 4, very pretty. The little pink orchid is still not out: but coming. Kind regards to your sister & much love from

yrs aff
H B Heelis

Got piano upstairs. My mother still searching! at present for title deeds & several sets of old teeth, and a black bag, and a book of Braile [sic] writing and various other things!

The 3/ stamps are for your p.orders, cashed.

Sawrey,
Ambleside
Aug 23.24

My dear Miss Choyce

I have kept intending to answer your letter, but I have been so *bothered* with the hay, the weather gets worse, it is a week since we had any carted. There has only been about ½ cart really spoilt, it is too cold weather to go mouldy; but it is wearisome work. And everybody gets irritable. Brockbank has gone to Ulverston hospital for an operation for piles, pretty severe, he had waited till he got into a bad state; but should be much better for it. Little Tommy Stevens has had his nose done, and little Florence Benson has had appendicitis successfully; so there has been a run on the Ulverston doctor.

Our corn is ripe and full of phaesants [sic]. I hope there may be a fine day to cut it when we get clear of St Swithin. [Rain or the absence of rain on St Swithin's day, 15 July, is said to presage the same for forty days.] You must excuse my writing, I have been chopping & shearing at Hill Top! let loose Tom Ch^son. [Christopherson] with a bill hook & a saw! I think of putting in low growing azaleas to choke the weeds another year. It looks quite tidy & clipped but slightly bare; we took out those broom bushes. The roses & honeysuckle have made plenty of new wood. I think the (grafted) lilacs want replacing also the apples on the walls; time passes; they have been in 18 years. I am expecting the George Heelis's on Monday, Mrs H. is not coming. The girl will be rather over doing, she improved very much with going to school but she is so enormous which she cannot help – I would much rather have had Esther. I am bothered about Nancy. She keeps having swolen [sic] glands. Her mother thinks the climate at Darlington does not suit her. It is an excellent school, and I doubt if climate makes much difference; but if there is the least risk of tuberculosis it would be better to face the situation, and send her to open air training for an outdoor life.

You sound to be having a lively time!

Do you remember the little creeping plant, it *had* a yellow broomlike flower when it came out. The tall yellow loosestrife is in flower now.

You have a habit of writing all ends up! I was tearing up an old letter of yours when what should I find but a belated – overlooked – request for a comfy bed!! I never saw it till lately. There was only one decent single bed disposable. I sent it to poor old Filkin at Sunderland. You may have thought it strange I never referred to your letter. I am very sorry your mother has been suffering so much, it is a cruel trial. My mother keeps very well and lively, she is wonderful. I must stop, I have several letters to write. Hope you do well at college, give my very kind regards to Mrs Lowson. We looked with much interest at the public school shootings at Bisley. [Denys Lowson was in the Winchester School shooting team and later was to shoot for Oxford against Cambridge, Harvard and Yale.]

With love yrs aff
Beatrix Heelis

Sawrey
Nr Ambleside
Feb 12th 25

My dear Miss Choyce,
    You seem to be having a troublesome time – cheer up! all times get over. Not that I mean to be unsympathetic. Cleaning boots "before supper" does not sound very reasonable. When are you coming to see us again? not that it matters *when* – for you are always welcome, and after last May's experience on[e] cannot call one month's weather any better than another. It has been an exceedingly wet wild winter, no frost to speak of. Today we are having snow showers with sunshine between; very sloshy. I am looking forward to going to the Grasmere play this afternoon, I asked my mother to lend her closed car as she would not be going out. She keeps very well but has not got over here regularly on account of the weather. I was really alarmed with the ferry last Sunday, it swung like a swing, such rolling waves. There was a concert last week at Bowness I would have liked to hear, but could not face the long drive round at night; did you ever hear the "Kennedy Fraser's" "Songs of the Hebrides"? one played the harp. Paterson, my mother's gardiner [sic], went and was delighted, he was able to understand the Gaelic. They have published some of the songs that they have collected; I think I will write and ask whether any of them have translated words.
    By the way I heard some of those nursery rhyme records the other day on the gramophone; it made me laugh remembering how you "took off" that man's nosey twang. The most tolerable was the 10 little niggers because the manner was less out of place in that ditty!
    I have been having a holiday from A.J.H. we sent him to the Nursing Home at Bowness "for Christmas" and then the flue [sic] was so bad in this village that we made it an excuse to leave him there a bit longer. I don't

look forward to having him back in this weather. The influenza has raged, but not in a severe type. Old Sam Postlethwaite, W. Possy's uncle has died, but he was 88; another elderly man was "given up" but he is recovering. Us & the farm, (touch wood) & the inn are the only houses that have escaped! We had colds earlier on, so I begin to hope we are going to keep clear. The Mackereths are all well. I don't think you have "reckoned up" Jenny. She is a very nice young woman and excellent confectioner, but she has little work in her. I don't think it is lazyness; she is not robust; Mrs M. can outstay Jenny and Belle (her md daughter) combined; and does not hesitate so to say, audibly! Jenny would not see me in a fix if I were in difficulty. So far it has answered very well having Mrs Rogerson daily instead of Mary. She is a far better servant and so much pleasanter than the girl. Mary was not able to come home for a weekend as expected at New Year because the children of the house where she is under housemaid had scarlet fever, slight but of course it put all in quarantine.

I have just been interrupted by a call from Mrs Crowly & the blind girl; she dropped a hint that Mrs Macpherson is expecting. Miss Hammond & Miss Mills are gone away for 2 months [they had rented the next door cottage from Beatrix since April 1922], their little dog is [to] stay here in the meantime; well behaved but rather petted.

The snap shots are very interesting. *Very* good of Denys and Mrs Lowson; a sad change in Mr Lowson, puffy and invalidish he looks as though he had had a stroke. It is excellent of Norma & the baby; but she is losing her looks. Little Joan is charming in the pansy frock, in the other one she has shut her little mouth like a mouse trap! And Kathleen has the sun in her eyes but they give a much better idea of the children than any you have sent before. I see you watching Joan from under a tree!

I cut out this piece about the sword dance from the Yorkshire Post. There was also a good deal about Co ops. I was glad it was given so much prominence. The meeting of the central Co op. association was simply red socialism and freedom of discussion not allowed. Shortly after there was a meeting of the Leeds branch which stopped the subsidy by a large majority. The societies appear to deal with the central society but I do not think that the majority of country co ops, like the Hawkshead shop, are in any way controlled by it, or subscribers to any levy.

It *is* sad to think of your mother and your brother John; it makes the future very unsettled for you, while she lasts. It sounds as though she were getting worse, if she requires the treatment so often. It is very sad that nothing can be done.

Thank you for the list of books, we had Laycock of Lonedale [by William Riley], a very pleasant old fashioned wholesome story. The trouble with Smith's library is that they don't send what is asked for. I must stop & make arrangements for deserting the menagerie this afternoon. Much love to you, and a kiss to Joan and to Kathleen.

Yrs aff
Beatrix Heelis

Sawrey
May 2.25

My dear Miss Choyce,

I was very glad to get your letter – both for itself and *your*self – also for its coming by return of post! Directly I had posted to *you*, expecting you the last week in May, Mr Heelis said perhaps he could get a short week off the office at Whitsuntide; so now that you have suggested June 8th it is quite clear that it will not clash – I couldn't and wouldn't have gone if you had just arrived. Now I will write a diplomatic letter to inquire after my Scotch sister-in-law's lambs [Beatrix's brother, Bertram, had died in 1918 and his widow, Mary, was continuing to run the farm in Ancrum on the Borders]. It is five or six years since I have been to Ashyburn; I do not wish to hurt her feelings, and they are less difficult to talk to on their "native heath" – not that there [is] heather; it is a pastoral country, with valleys & green hills. In [another] way June would suit me. I had a letter from Nancy's mother after writing to you. She is having treatment by inocculation [sic] till the end of May and will not be going back to school next term. I have wanted to see her for a long time, to see what she is like since she grew out of a child, and I should like to get her over while you are here. You have had more experience and judgement of young persons than I have. As regards her health I should simply put her under the observation of the District Nurse, like she has been at Kirkby Thore. (Where things are in a poor way I am afraid.) It is very perplexing. If poor Nancy is not going to be strong enough to work, and the family are going to have to live in a cottage, it seems to me it might be better to send her to an open air school at the sea side for the good of her health, rather than to spend any more on advanced education; and let her do the h usework & garden afterwards – I doubt if there is much opening for paid women agriculturalists & gardeners since the war. I cannot see much advantage in sending her to an agricultural college [Nancy Hudson, née Nicholson, was still going strong in 1994 at the age of eighty-five]. Your brother Tom's experience of gardening outlook is discouraging. What a very good idea to learn to drive, it will give him a far better chance.

It sounds as if your work was cut out! Your garden is very much more forward than here; except that we have some early potatoes showing; they are black! Peas also are being eaten by mice. I consider it is a very late spring, unless things come with a rush. How sad it is to hear of your mother's pain; and nothing can stop it. Poor thing it is a martyrdom. You cannot be decided at all about dates, and plans while she is suffering. When you [know?] you can come let me know and I will send the fare; [do?] please Choycey if Nancy is here it will be a reason for a fee; I didn't last time because you were on a holiday between work at a post, but you may easily be unsettled for a time if your mother's health gets worse rather than better[.] If I go away at Whitsuntide I shall shut up the house, I'm sure Miss Mills would look after the poultry – also the widow Christopherson is coming to the back cottage at the Castle, as the Bibbys have taken a farm. It will be convenient to have Tom near at hand to look after animals here. He comes in Sunday mornings which Brockbank never did except as a favour. The Bibbys are going to Coniston at May term. It is still very cold and showery.

With love yrs aff
Beatrix Heelis

'Peas also are being eaten by mice.'

In the next letter Beatrix is confused about the Heelis family. There were eleven children, Willie being the youngest and Edward Alexander (known by the family as 'Alec') the oldest son, born in 1858 after three girls. Beatrix is also wrong in naming Hugh as Alec's 'next brother'. There were two boys in between, William Ernest (who died when very young) and Arthur John.

Sawrey
July 27.25

Dear Miss Choyce

Thank you for your kind letter. The brother who has died is not the favourite-next-youngest brother George – he was the eldest of the long family of 10 – Alic [sic] – the head of the family. His death is a disappointment rather than a shock. He has been in bad health for nearly two years with the prospect of a severe but not hopeless operation hanging over him. He went twice to Manchester at several months interval but his heart was not strong enough – on the third occasion the operation was performed very successfully and he got home alright, but died suddenly, sitting in his chair. I think the terrific heat may have had something to do with it, it was extraordinary last week, our therm^{tr} was 122 in the sun on Friday & 85 in shade. The welcome rain & thunder came on Saturday night; it was very awkward, everything burnt up & so short of water.

Alic leaves a grown up family, a nice daughter unmarried [Sylvie], a married son [Guy] & a younger boy [Hylton]. He was a big, silent, responsible sort of man, courteous and very deaf. I had seen him 3 or 4 times when I was at Appleby, but scarcely knew him. The next brother Hugh I have never met! He is a bit cranky owing to an accident to his skull, married & lives in Northumberland. I should think we shall be having Rosemary & Colin later. I trust *not* Mrs G! Their father may be detained at home by business. Wm has gone to the funeral today. Give my love to your dear mother, and with love to yourself

yrs aff
Beatrix Heelis

Sawrey
Oct 16.25

My dear Miss Choyce

Is not this Cornish heath? I was so surprised to find it, but I hasten to explain that I doubt if it is native. There is a plant growing inside that circle of wire netting where I have rhodoadendrons [sic] near the tarn, I should think the seed got in along with the alpine rhododendron, the heath is sometimes grown by nurserymen. The pears arrived beautifully packed, they look as if they will be of the melting-in-your-mouth description when ripe. I have them in the sun on the window. If they are as good as the apples they will be a treat. It is a lovely day, snow on Coniston, but melted quickly with the sun. We have got a nice lot of bracken. Now the mangolds are being lifted, not large, but useful. There was a white frost last night, the dahlias are blacked. I am still planting bulbs, they ought to be all in, the snowdrops are poking their noses through already. Had we a hatch of ducklings when you were here, from Mrs Fowkes' ducks. They are in the orchard opposite the Castle, and so wild we cannot catch them. Mr Heelis *shot* the biggest drake, rather a ghastly job. I am glad Nurse will be back next week. A.J.H. is much the same, complains of the colder weather. I am glad you can give a little better account of your mother, but I fear at the best – it is sad enough; give her my love. The baby across the road sounds to be a little dear. I am glad you have pleasant young neighbours, for cheerfulness. I had a contented letter from Nancy, she likes the school and she is spending a lot of time out of doors. I hope that does not mean that the gland is troublesome again, perhaps it is a precaution on the part of the school mistress.

Now I must get in a few more bulbs.

With love & many thanks for the pears yrs aff
Beatrix Heelis

The next letter is undated but it is written on the same distinctive lined paper of the previous letter. The cupboard mentioned (and illustrated) still stands in Hill Top, opposite the kitchen range, on the right as you enter through the front door.

[?1925]

My dear Miss Choyce,

Have I a-fool-of-myself-at-a-sale-made? I do not know, I cannot tell! The advt in the Gazette announced several cows, an aged black mare £2.10.0 a calf, hay mows etc etc and "a portion of household furniture". It was at a little out of the way farm near Crook, a forlorn dirty little place, everyone dead except an old man removed to the infirmary. My purpose was to buy the calf, a nice little red heifer, which we obtained for £3 and stowed into the back seat of the car. I poked into a dark dirty little kitchen and amongst broken chairs & lumber beheld a carved & dated dark oak court cupboard. I suppose it had been too lumbersome to remove with the other "portion of household furniture." I had vain hopes that I was going to get a bargain – no dealers. But there is no such thing as bargains in this district; there appeared two other knowledgeable people – a second auctioneer R D Dickerson and an unknown lady & gentleman; between them I paid 21.10. If it is rubbish when it arrives I will tear up this letter! Unquestionably it is genuine & untouched – except by rats. It did not seem to be wormy. The back was eaten into holes.

There was a nice small gate legged oak table but it wanted a flap. It was bought for £2 by the man who keeps the Beech hill hotel. I hope & trust foot & mouth is not going to spread, the outbreak in South Lancs has caused consternation. I expect nothing else but that Westmorland will (sensibly but inconveniently) close the bridges. I shall be in a nice hole with sheep if they do. I was alright today bringing a calf from West^d to Lancs across the ferry. The weather is wild; but the woods are still very lovely. There are showers like thunder rain.

I am glad your mother is fairly comfortable, I will post you either a chicken or a rabbit next week.

Yrs aff.
Beatrix Heelis

I don't know much about oak. The doors fastened with little wooden buttons. The carving was rather rough. Possibly the piece may at some time have been fixed in a wall, it had a deal back. It had belonged to the aged wife, the neighbours said she had refused good offers in her lifetime for the "sideboard".

Did I tell you we have had 12 bull calves, to only one female?

[Written in pencil by BP] I think it is a very good cupboard, horribly dirty, but it will polish alright, except for some clumpsy later date hinges, and a drop corner damaged it is in good condition.

I must keep away from sales for some time!

There is another long break in the correspondence here, during which Arthur John died. On 9 January 1926 Beatrix wrote to Fruing Warne, 'Our poor invalid Arthur Heelis has peacefully fallen asleep. It is a release for him & will be a relief when one gets used to it.'

There is no clue in any of the two hundred or so of Beatrix's letters written between 1925 and 1933, that we have, as to whether Louie Choyce continued to be a regular summer visitor to Sawrey, but the tone of the next letter leads me to believe that the two women had certainly kept in close touch.

During the gap in the correspondence Beatrix had been entertaining an increasing number of visitors from America, notably Mrs Templeman Coolidge and her son, Henry P., and the publisher, Alexander McKay. David McKay of Philadelphia published THE FAIRY CARAVAN *in October 1929 and Beatrix dedicated the book to Henry P. In January 1930 Beatrix bought the 5,000 acre Monk Coniston Estate, and in September 1930* THE TALE OF LITTLE PIG ROBINSON *was published by both David McKay and Frederick Warne. Louie's mother had died in 1926 at the age of seventy-five and Beatrix's mother on 20 December 1932 at the age of ninety-three.*

Castle Cottage,
Sawrey
Nov 1.33

My dear Miss Choyce,

I *have* been busy, as usual; and I have often remarked if the weather kept fine for 12 months on end – there would be several things left undone the last fortnight – including drains, re-slating of roofs, and especially the digging up and replanting of flower borders. I thought I was getting on with the last job in early October, but it is not half finished, and the bulbs are too advanced to take up now. You know our garden is carpeted [sic] with snowdrops. I got most of Hill Top dug up with assistance, it was in a great mess.

This spring summer & autumn has been a treat, a wonderful season, and we were never parched nor short of water here. I have seen the grass much more burnt in ordinary summers on shallow rocky pastures. Still – we were all very glad when the rain came, because there was no demand for sheep or cattle to go elsewhere. But there has been a great improvement in prices, the last fair on Oct 28th was 6/ or 8/ up, our best herdwick lambs made 22/ compared with 13/ last year. I hope the corner has been turned at last. There is much controversy over the milk job. [On 6 October a milk pooling system came into operation in England and Wales. Milk was graded into three categories and sold at prices fixed by the Milk Marketing Board.] I registered on receiving the notice, but am glad to say I have heard nothing further. I think it was a pity to apply it to retail trade – Milk has been raised 2d at Kendal; from 5d to 7d per quart, and sales are about halved. Of course people can perfectly well afford a copper or two; but they won't, and the children suffer. We don't come under it as we sell less than a gallon outside self & servants families. The fairs & shows are over, except one bull sale, we want to buy a new bull, a black galloway, to replace one that is 3 year old. The crops were good and haymaking was a pleasure, and so soon over we could go to shows with a clear conscience, the sheep took a lot of tickets.

I hope I shall see you when you come to Outgate; and I hope you will have decent weather! It is "clashy" at present, very cold rough showers, & rather apt to give people colds. We are alright so far.

I used a weed killer for the first time at Hill Top in the stone paving, it was said to be non arsenical and probably *was* harmless – it did *not* kill deep rooted weeds!

I remain yrs aff
Beatrix Heelis

'We want to buy a new bull...'

Amongst the letters from Beatrix to Louie there is one dated Apr 7 34, but I am suspicious about the date for a number of reasons and believe that Beatrix meant to write '35'. 1) In the next letter (12 April) Beatrix apologises for answering Louie's letter 'at last', when she had apparently written to her only five days previously. 2) In the 7 April letter Beatrix writes, 'The daffodils will be over before Easter'. In 1934 Easter was on 1 April, but in 1935 Easter was on 21 April. 3) In the 7 April letter Beatrix refers to the death of her favourite ewe, Queenie, and writing to her shepherd, Joseph Moscrop, on 30 March 35 she tells him that ' "Hill Top Queenie" is very bad . . .'. The same letter relates that 'the grass has come with a rush', and the 7 April letter to Louie mentions that 'The spring grass came with such a rush 10 days ago'. 4) The 7 April letter tells Louie of plans for a village celebration with a bonfire 'on the height above Hill Top'. In May 1935 the country celebrated the Silver Jubilee of King George V with bonfires and tea parties.

The letter written on 7 April can now be found on page 53.

The letter written on 7 April can now be found on page 53.

Castle Cottage
Sawrey
Nr Ambleside
Ap. 12. 34

Dear Miss Choyce,

I take the opportunity of a very wet day and a cold to answer your letter at last. The rain is very welcome but the cold could have been dispensed with. I have no luck this winter. Whenever I feel very well again – something goes wrong. I had an awful shaking up when I put my shoulder out. I can get my hand on top of my head now, so I hope there will be no permanent stiffness. I fell over a board in a door way.

The change of weather since yesterday is delightful; it can turn cold again as there has been thunder and lightning, but there is a good soak anyway. We have not been short of water; but very short of grass. There are 37 lambs here; they should be coming on most of the high farms this weekend, so the rain is just in time. The wild daffodils are out but not the garden varieties yet. I am afraid there will be scarcely any blossom; a pair of bullfinches have lived in the garden all winter, continually stripping the damsons & gooseberries & currants. They are very pretty, but they really want shooting, whether protected or not. There seems to be a lot of mole hills, I thought it was because the mole catcher has retired, but perhaps it is the season.

The artless homely poem is very pleasing, a genuine heartfelt description of a real English homestead, it is very much to your credit to be so cheerful after leaving behind such a beautiful happy home. Things have to pass away; and I am afraid in this country such a world will never come back. Perhaps it may still exist in the colonies. It is a pleasant memory.

I thought of our singing games last Saturday when I was in Keswick and overheard some little girls puzzling out a half forgotten skipping rhyme. I doubt if even *you* could make the present generation of Sawrey children do singing games. The Folk dancing goes on; but I have my doubts! They are getting too prone to exhibition dancing, especially too much morris. Some rivalry and emulation between centres is stimulating. But the real essence of folk dancing is that all 'folk' should dance and dance for enjoyment, not for showing off, young & old, rich & poor, good & indifferent dancers. Too much morris means that all the older & shy dancers sit out, & sneeze. I saw a pleasant dance the other night, 'Newcastle' one never tires of. A set of 6 Sawrey girls did the sticks morris – is it Lads a bunchin? – perfectly – but I consider it is only exceptionally compact light girls, such as Ethel Green, who look really well in Morris dancing. The Class were hesitating whether to go to the entertainment because they had no "new" dance to show off – what nonsense! Mr Heelis said he would get up a company of old fat ones to dance Newcastle if the others would not, so they went. I have missed most of the winter dance evenings but hope to go to the Grasmere festival.

Your garden will be coming on. We are late here, sadly behindhand with getting peas in etc.

Shall I send the little poem back? or keep it. I really value it. Mr Heelis liked it, which was a compliment, as he despises poetry!! He said the 1st verse was a crib. "I remember I remember the house where I was born, T. Hood.

But the other verses are not so –

Yrs aff
Beatrix Heelis

Castle Cottage
Sawrey
nr Ambleside
Oct 20th 34

Dear Miss Choyce,

After some search I found the right morris [dance] book – alas there is nobody to play them! I put on the gramophone records occasionally. I hope I may get to some of the pleasant parties this winter; last year I was not well, one thing or other – but have felt unusually fit the last six months (touch wood!) I don't know how we survive through such a climate. Except one interval of very fine hot 4 days in September I really don't think there have been 2 days together without rain since the weather broke on St Swithin's. Each month is worse than the month before. The autumn colours would be lovely if the sun shone.

On the whole it is maybe well that your visit waits till spring, though I am *very* sorry for the reason. I know it will be a worry to you, and serious for your brother. It seems so difficult to find posts. My mother's gardiner [sic] was out of work after Lindeth How was sold, at last he is gradually getting jobbing work in Windermere. It is a great pity after your brother being so comfortably settled.

I hope you had an interesting day yesterday 20th to cheer you up. How valuable the Kelmscott books continue, I see in an advt. catalogue the Chaucer quoted at £250.

The Sawrey folk dance class has started again for the winter, 18 members. Several children come in, having left school. The choral society is also alive and squalling, but they cannot agree about a conductor. They practiced [sic] here once a week last winter which no doubt was good for the piano. I think they try to do too difficult music, for their main efforts. The Kendal festival takes place again next year, they wanted Bach but some of the villagers won't.

I am glad your garden has given you satisfaction, ours was very dried up and then too cold and wet. The second row of peas never provided a single dish. But it is best row of celery ever grown here. There are plenty of apples. Plum blossom was destroyed last spring by the bullfinches, they have become a perfect nuisance, they stripped the buds from the currant & gooseberry bushes too.

The sheep fairs are an improvement, quite 3/ a head up since a year ago. My half bred lambs averaged over £1 per head, top price 26/- There was one terrible season when top price was 12/!! But Herdwick wool sticks at

4d and I doubt if it will ever rise much because its main use was for making carpets – now everyone has parquet or linoleum. I am told by American friends that there is scarcely a carpet to be seen in U.S.A., where our wool used to go. It cannot be helped. The poor sheep have to be clipped in summer.

My flock has taken a great many prizes at the local shows – over forty this summer, mainly for female sheep. But I have had to give back the champion cup; a young farmer from Grasmere has *one* ewe which beats my younger ewes, though I regularly beat him with a pair. Our old "Waterlily" is still alive and has reared another prize win[n]ing lamb; but I insisted on retiring her last year, as I could see she was embarrassing to the judges! still the best sheep; but too ancient. She has bred a family of over a dozen descendants, all show specimens. Lately I have been amused with the rearing of a family of pups, from my own favourite colley [sic]; two of them are now out to work, but the baby of the family is a handful. She learns tricks like a monky [sic]; but I perceive I shall have to harden my heart and give her a thrashing.

Did I tell you Colin Heelis has been home from the Argentine, for first holiday, after 5 years. He has gone back for another 5. He is doing well, on the railway, and not a bit changed or worsened. His cousin Esther Nicolson was over from NZ two years ago and has also gone back. She got a post & stayed a year, but she said she preferred N.Z. for teaching – she says when she can retire she would prefer the old country.

Mr Heelis's eldest sister [Blanche] is failing, at Appleby, she is nearly 80; they were a long family. Wm. is very well and not deaf. Rather tied up with work, and he says it invariably rains every Saturday afternoon & Sunday. There are not much changes lately in the village, only old Mr Edmondson is dead at Brynswood at top of the Ferry hill. The family are anxious to sell, I suppose it will mean another large empty house.

Do you ever see the "Countryman". I have given up taking it, I think the advts are so irritating and it is rather a south country periodical. If you have not had it I will send you the last year's 4 vols.

I wish you had not had this anxiety, I do hope your brother will be lucky in finding a new post.

Yrs aff.
Beatrix Heelis

Castle Cottage
Sawrey
Dec 20th. 34

My dear Miss Choyce

What a pretty little tea cloth you have sent me – did you work it I wonder? It will be useful as most of mine are too big. (Commercial traveller interrupted at door) I *cannot* remember if I have sent you the card, and it would be so shocking to forget you that I had better risk sending twice. I have still letters to write so must stop – We have had a really sunny day after much rain & fog.

By the way I must write one word more, I was rather glad you had *not* gone to Oxford. I don't think yours is the right temperament for the Oxford Group – at least you are *too* much suitable – you are rather highly strung; and you have never seemed to me to be so desperately wicked as to require spectacular "saving"! The people at the Garth went rather crazy over it. When it came to that rather conceited child Meg going about to save grown-ups, I thought it was silly; and impertinent; though well meant. Like the Salv. Army it can do great service in bad cases; but it can send quite decent christians silly.

Keep away from the group and do village folk dancing.

Yrs aff.
H B Heelis

Castle Cottage
Sawrey
Ap. 7. 34

Dear Miss Choyce,

I do not know what to think. I think with Mr Baldwin it is unfortunate that flying was ever invented. I have always thought the League of Nations is a humbug. If this nation had stood aside and kept up the tradition of a British navy it might have been a better prospect for civilization in the long run, even if it sounded selfish in the present. If the European countries choose to destroy each other – I only hope we can keep out of it, for it is doubtful if we could do much good. Without being a pacificist [sic] it seems rather wicked, as well as foolish, to contemplate the possibility of joining with other nations in a threat to bomb any aggressor. It would be asking for an air raid on London. The peace ballot was a humbug. It is curious how little has been said about the result. The only newspaper comment I have read was in a local paper which said it was a complete fiasco. The majority was 88%, but only 23% of the electors voted in this district. I refused the paper offered to us; it might have been more strong minded to give ones reasons – but then it did seem too late to leave the league. I only wish it would collapse.

We have had a wet winter here, and never any heavy snow. March was mild and sun shining. The daffodils will be over before Easter. Last week was much colder and there were snow showers on Friday but it soon melted in the sun, and never lay on the low ground. Sheep have wintered well – Though we have had some distressing losses of favourites – my best favourite poor Queenie died last night, heavy with lamb. The spring grass came with such a rush 10 days ago it has caused losses amongst ewes on too rich pasture, blown up. They have wintered too well; over fat. Lambs are only beginning amongst the herdwick sheep. The half bred flocks seem to have plenty of twins.

What an awful price for coal! It must be very difficult for you to manage. What a tragedy it is when a man is willing to work and cannot get a post. I am sure it must be very worrying both for you and him [Louie's brother, Tom]. I am sorry to hear about gout in the eyes, my mother's mother Grandma Leech used to suffer from it, it is very painful.

Does not laurel grow with you? It is only leaves to sew into wreaths, or is it branches? Tom has a great heap to burn I was thinking it ought to go onto the bonfire. There is to be a fire on the height above Hill Top; a school tea & sports, its to be hoped it is a fine day. We have kept very well, there has been no flue of any moment, and I have not caught it. We did a little spring cleaning, but I cannot get hold of the painter, I want the stairs & landing done. The woods & hedges will burst into leaf with todays rain. We have *nothing* in! except the oats not even beans. We must get some peas sown. The bullfinches have become a great nuisance, especially stripping damson blossom.

With much love yrs aff.
Beatrix Heelis

Castle Cottage
Sawrey
nr Ambleside
July 20 35

Dear Miss Choyce,

We have been having experience of a rather peculiar visitor, (with a trustworthy introduction!) in fact personally conducted by a very old friend [Samuel Hamer, Secretary of the National [Trust], who considers the young man a musical genius. In case Mr [Christopher] Le Fleming achieves fame – he is worth describing – about 25–6, over 6 foot, short sighted, slight squint, ill made; not unpleasant looking, but 'gawky' and decidedly odd. With a pleasant sensible sandy haired wife a little older than himself. I barred inviting them here, in fact I was rather pleased to be full up with relations, so I lodged them out.

This young man has composed piano pieces, sufficiently simple for children – founded upon (what's the right term?) the Peter Rabbit books. inspired!!! When Mr Hamer wrote to me about him several months ago I said I thought it absurd; but he was welcome to communicate with my publishers (who are about as unmusical as me.) He got his compositions accepted by a music firm named Chesters [J. & W. Chester Ltd], & Messrs Warne showed willing. Then the pieces were to be played to *me* before going further – so they trailed up here. And were received as a joke. I don't know anything about music. The pieces seem to me to be perfectly charming; and what is more they do somehow suggest the theme. There is the little pitter pattering merry tune that he calls PR & Benj. B. and 5 others. Mrs Tiggy he has founded on "Lily white and clean oh". The puddleducks is the best – pit pat paddle pat. I think you would like them, they are very like the Folk dance music, catchy tunes, and very limpid tinkling music. The young man is a teacher of music, living near Ringwood in the New Forest. He can play with great execution, but he says himself not sufficiently well to make a living thereby, and his ambition is to be a composer. He has had some songs published. I am quite willing to do what I can by redrawing subjects in black & white as heading to his little pieces. He did not suggest any attempt to provide song words.

He has set some of the psalms as songs. One of them was really terrible, over powering. The piano survives. Another was the harps and cymbals and dancing. If it is any sign of genius I think he is a bit mad. He & wife and introducer departed to London this morning leaving us rather limp!! If he ever proposes another visitation I will get you over by providing a third class return and you could instruct him & his wife how to sing Flowers in the Vally [sic]; they made a sad hash of it. They did the lark in the morn rather well, only the lady had no voice compared with you. He sang one very pleasant song I do not remember to have heard before – its refrain was something like "And so round my hat I wear a willow bough".

I now come to my reason for writing – *have you got a book* that had some *children songs* in it? I thought I had, but cannot find any such. We adjourned to Possy's and Mary & Manda & I tried to remember singing games, with fair success, Mr Le Fleming is going to try to get another verse of the "Big Ship sails' he agrees with me that it is probably the chorus of a sea chanty. The point is that I have always wanted our Sawrey singing games written down because the tunes are different, and I think better than those in the book which I cannot find. He took notes and may make out something from them. I gave him a short acting piece that I made long ago out of Squirrel Nutkin, for the Brownies; into this I introduced singing games such as Nuts in May – also some bits of rhymes that I do not know music for – like the King of Spains Daughter. The young man took it away with him. I wish he could make a sort of little operetta, working in tunes, his own, and old ones. He fully appreciated folk songs. But he had next to no voice. Altogether it was a curious experience. I think there must be something in those psalm songs unpublished; they disconcerted the audience. He also imitated a tinkling musical box.

We had a grand *week* in the hay. Then drizzle since Wednesday, and last night thunder rain. If it does not mend there will be much hay spoilt up and down. We have 54 carts, over 30 to get, two fields wet.

I hope you are keeping alright, I don't like hearing of rheumatic pains. Stiff joints grow upon us.

I remain yrs aff
Beatrix Heelis

Christopher Le Fleming's two PETER RABBIT MUSIC BOOKS *were published jointly by J. W. Chester Ltd and Frederick Warne in December 1935, Book I containing 'Six Easy Pieces' and Book II 'Six Easy Duets', all for the piano. Beatrix provided a pencil sketch for the appropriate character to head each piece, intending to work on the final drawings when they had been approved. Due to a misunderstanding the sketches were inked over by an unknown hand and then printed. Beatrix commented to a friend, 'The result was better than might have been expected.'*

It was not until over thirty years later, in 1967, that the SQUIRREL NUTKIN *play was published by Warne, with the lengthy title* SQUIRREL NUTKIN, A CHILDREN'S PLAY ADAPTED BY BEATRIX POTTER FROM HER ORIGINAL STORY, MUSIC ADAPTED FROM TRADITIONAL TUNES BY CHRISTOPHER LE FLEMING.

All three books have been out of print for many years.

Castle Cottage
Sawrey
Nr Ambleside
Feb 4.36

Dear Miss Choyce,

I came to same conclusion after hearing about your chintz so I waited! I am writing to Morris's [William Morris's manufacturing and decorative firm] by this post ordering 3 of the Daisy. Do not spoil the job for want of a 4th piece. I sent all I had of the Daisy, I have some scraps more of the willow. The willow is a very beautiful design but I think the colour is just heavy, at least it fights with any pictures or ornaments; and conquers. As regards carpets you had better be content with art squares, and felt under, if too thin. My green Axminster cost £30, and I am always in fear of something being spilt on it. Good pile carpets are very dear. I don't care for cheap oriental myself, I prefer matting to Indian carpets.

I thought you might be interested and know some of the names at the funeral of Mr Kipling. What a loss; those two.

King George V had died on 20 January and his body brought from Sandring-ham to lie-in-state in London on 23 January. Rudyard Kipling had died on 18 January and six days later his ashes were placed in Poets' Corner, Westminster Abbey, next to those of Thomas Hardy and Charles Dickens. The service was broadcast to the nation and the list of mourners in The Times *took up three-quarters of a column. Among those present were Stanley Baldwin and his family and Kipling's literary agent, A. P. Watt.*

We went to St Mary's Church Ambleside to hear the funeral, thinking it would be solemn and a *good wireless* in the parish church, whereas it was very badly tuned. Fine, and wonderful to hear the guns and the wailing of the bagpipes. But the interruptions of a very loud announcer were irritating. Also I was sitting waiting opposite the most atrocious stain glass memorial window, with forget me nots as large as cabbages and colour to match.

We have very hard frost and a little fresh snow, it is a bad time for sheep and out door work at a stand still.

I remain, yrs aff
Beatrix Heelis

The National Trust had appointed a new Land Agent, Bruce Thompson, and Beatrix had been showering him with advice and practical information in four lengthy letters written since 1 January.

Castle Cottage
Sawrey
nr Ambleside
Jan 31.37

Dear Miss Choyce,

What will you think of me not thanking you for the dear little brooch and your loving remembrance? I have been in a slow muddle of letter writing for so long; trying to over take various business as well as Christmas letters. I hope to post a phaesant [sic] tomorrow – Monday – as a peace offering. Mr Heelis has not had much shooting; he was upset about poor George Milligan's death early on; and what with wet Saturdays etc. the shooting has been under a cloud this year. We have escaped flue so far – It has been very bad in Winderemere, Ambleside and Hawkshead but the first cases are only beginning in Sawrey. Not that I think there is more or less risk through its being in this village – one runs against it in every other house or shop. Nephew Jack had a sudden sharp attack; no one else in the office. Wm. has had a tiresome hanging on head cold for several weeks. In other respects we are still very well. We should be thankful we have only had a sprinkling from the recent snowstorm elsewhere. But we are *not* thankful for anything appertaining to the weather; it has been a horrid winter, usually wet and a gale; but between times bitterly cold for a day or two. It has spared the hay. The cattle have been out a lot. The hay is plentiful, but poor, not much good for keeping up butterfats. There seems to be a feeling of unrest in the farming world. Too much interference; well meant; unavoidable; but unsettling and very expensive. Undoubtedly the ulterior motive behind all this organizing is co ordination of supplies for defence. The motive is all to the good, but it is expensive to work; and the farming industry is getting irritated with all this spectacle of highly paid officials.

I never knew tenants so unsettled up here. It is disappointing, in face of a strong rise in wool. I sold at 6½d and it has got up to 10d in five months. Yet men are wanting to give up sheep farming and turn to *milk*; although the dairy farmers grumble too.

The snowdrops are nearly full out in the garden. Has anything been done about your drains? I wish Denys would happen to call while there is a flood on! The rain has commenced again since I started this letter; there is a lot of snow on the fells, so the Brathay will be a fine sight.

There are great changes at Grizedale; old Mr Harold Brocklebank died, and his son is making himself highly disagreeable. No doubt he is sore about death duties. To our amusement the innocent W.H and J.H. have an intimation – in his own hand – to say that all fishing leave is withdrawn. Tiddlers; 8 inch; with a worm. The fishing will not be missed! He has turned the servants adrift except one rabbit trapper. No one believes he is as badly off as all that. I wonder what will happen to his sheep if there is much snow. The Hellicars are leaving, going to Ipswich, their native county. Her relations are in business, at docks or something; he will get employment, but they are taking it very hard. Unfortunately hard, and almost foolishly, for they must have known – or should have guessed – what was likely to happen. Mr Arthur Brocklebank disliked Grizedale. It is a dull place, it will be bad to sell.

I remain with love yr aff.

Beatrix Heelis

Castle Cottage
Sawrey
Ap. 22.37

My dear Miss Choyce,

I am sorry you have been poorly, and I sympathize, I had a turn in March, too, the doctor said it was something I had eaten, it made me very sore inside but I soon recovered. I hope you are better and able to enjoy this "droppy" April, real good growing weather for grass & lambs, though still cold in the north. Very risky weather for chills. One of the little pekes has had inflammation, but recovered with a mustard poultice [in 1936 Beatrix had acquired two Pekinese puppies which she called Tzusee (Susie) and Chuleh (Julie)]. The lambs are a good crop, in spite of the terrible privations which the sheep endured in March. The blizzard on March 1st was the worst that this generation of shepherds had experienced. Many drifts will remain till summer. There was plenty of grass blown bare, but repeated snow showers hungered the sheep. We lost perhaps 30, perhaps more, when the drifts disappear. They were caught suddenly when rain changed to snow on Saturday afternoon 28th Feb. It was too dark to go up the fell and next morning the snow was to the top of the back windows of many farms. Our men got out about 400 between

Sunday aft. and Wednesday – mostly no worse. There have been many tiresome nesses – Some seasons are like that! The Sanitary inspector – a new broom – is making things difficult. It is a new experience to be reported as a slum landlord. I think it is shortsighted policy in a district that depends so much on the picturesque. He has condemned one of my cottages where the indignant old woman says she has never once had a doctor in 40 years. She may last a good while, but it is not to be relet after she is gone. The man told someone that half Hawkshead wants demolishing. Some of it wants using for store rooms or such like, but the new cottages won't stand like the old ones. I am more than sorry to hear that your brother is unsettled again – get him to do the digging for you. It is grievous how the old set are going from this changing world. I think Newbery Choyce was a magnificent sonnet writer. I missed his obituary in the Times – and I missed cutting out one about the last Miss Macdonald – Lady Burne Jones's [sic] last surviving sister. Mr Baldwyn [sic] going – it won't bear thinking of! but he does look so tired. [After becoming Prime Minister for the third time in June 1935, seventy-year-old Stanley Baldwin had announced his resignation, which would take place on 28 May 1937. Miss Edith Macdonald, Baldwin's aunt, had died on 30 March at the age of eighty-eight. The last of five sisters, she had lived in the Baldwin family house for sixty years.] Perhaps even from a selfish point of view it is better. Let him rest, in case he were wanted in extremity. But I think his firmness will have saved the situation. There was a striking sentence in a letter from an American friend who said 'We think England rearming is the best guarantee for peace''. I am sure you must feel the losses of these friends.

With love yrs aff
Beatrix Heelis

Castle Cottage
Sawrey
Aug 28.37

My dear Miss Choyce,

I believe I owe you reply to 2 letters – I don't know where time runs to, at this time of year, the days seem more full than ever. It has been lovely weather, we have finished our small harvest this evening, untouched by rain except a few drops one morning. Most of the abundant hay crop is equally good. Two fields here were rather spoilt, being out a fortnight, but so much good was got before and after that it is not serious. Today I have had the novel experience of acting as co-judge at Lowick Show, for the classes of Herdwick sheep, and colley [sic] dogs – dear dogs I would have liked to give prizes to half a dozen instead of 3. The sheep were only a moderate exhibit, as it is too far down country at Lowick, between the lower end of Coniston lake and the Greenod[d] sands – a pretty drive and fine day. The other judge was an elderly farmer, a good lead.

On Thursday we went to Cockermouth show beyond Keswick, a fine view, plenty of entries, *and* an enjoyable day. The ewes got another cup (year only). I have one cup won outright, and 2 others held for this season (only) by the same ram. He is a beauty, but I doubt if he will grow sufficiently big to win in an old class next year. I did not know Sawrey boasted an athlete since the Hoggarth boy ceased to compete in the boy's race – who is the name of Simms? It takes an outsider to hear the news! The gossip you have heard is correct that I have bought the small Belmount estate and another piece, but Miss Owen continues at Belmount Hall & garden – I cannot imagine her or me turning it into flats; one drawback is that there is no water supply except rain water. We have been a bit short here; but there is usually a break, or thunder rain, before the last gasp. There was too much rain in spring for the garden, it never got weeded and it is an overgrown tangle. Plums set in profusion, but since the dry weather they are falling off unripe, very sticky blight. There is a good crop of potatoes. Apples sufficient; there were more than enough last year. It will be nice to hear the folk music on the *piano* again. At the dance festival at Grasmere they had music relaid [sic] through an awful loud speaker. It may have been satisfactory to dance to, but the effect to me was utterly mechanical and odious – I would rather listen to human wrong notes!. I wonder if the Morris dancers will come round again this year. We keep very well – no younger [Beatrix was seventy-one]. It is very bad luck that you should have that invasion all round, I hear of someone else in the same plight with a newly bought house in Somerset, there seems no remedy, unless to let the house to the military.

With love yrs aff.
Beatrix Heelis.

After a short stay in the Women's Hospital, Catharine Street, Liverpool, the previous November, Beatrix had to return there at the end of March. She had a serious operation early in April.

Sawrey
May 10th. 39

Dear Miss Choyce,

Thank you for your letter and the book – a wonderful genius and an iron constitution. She seems to have had the same understanding and influence over Asiatics as Laurence [sic] of Arabia, without the self consciousness which makes his writings a little irritating.

It is about as warm as the Tropics now, but we are not properly thankful for lovely weather – it is like last May – far too dry. There was some thunder & rain last Saturday, only for a day.

I came home by road Sunday week, and can now hobble about with a stick. Which I am told is good progress. You repeat the chorus of "glad to get home". Am I cross grained? or does it not occur to people that when one is seriously ill & quite unable to [to] be attending to things (everything a bother!) it is to my thinking *far pleasanter* to be right away, out of it all. There could not be a pleasanter place to be ill in. I have been twice in Catharine Street hospital, and both times I have been heartily sorry to leave! only it is selfish to want to hold up a bed. I hope after Sunday I shall be able to do for myself indoors. As for the garden it is an outfacing mess, full of plants that I meant to have lifted and devided [sic] last winter.

Some apple blossom beginning to show pink; pear in full flower; plum over. The daffys are over and the wild hyacinths out, also wild cherries, there is no hawthorn blossom. It is a pity W. Steevens [sic] is such a hop[e]less fool in a garden. He has not the recognising to take up docks & dandelions; but he has scraped the "weathering" & moss off the outdoor stairs including a little saxifrage which I valued; no sense and does not listen either.

Mrs Edwards [the nurse] is here till Sunday. I am in the upstairs sitting room & she is in the spare room. I can now get in and out of bed. I got a small bed in Liverpool that "racks up". I have always sneered at married people requiring 2 beds! but now don't know what to do. W.H. is an uneasy bed fellow, in the habit of rolling up the whole of the bedclothes – so much so that the last three winters I have hit on the plan of having a thick separate rug. There is not room for 2 beds in our old bedroom and the spare room is bitterly cold in winter, perhaps it will be better to sleep in the piano. It is a pleasant outlook.

Whether this end of the house will be – or will not be – wanted for refugee cousins is past telling. Apart from the horrid suspense – what awful waste of time, energy, and money.

I wonder if Tom will be accepted? [War with Germany seemed inevitable and on 27 April conscription had been announced in Britain for men aged 20 and 21.] What annoys me is the way young people are *not* taken, just like last time – crowds of idle lads who ought for their own good and other peoples good – to be drilled and disciplined. Why are they not all drilled for a couple of years after leaving school? Its a most annoying world to come back into – home and foreign! big and little! I sit under the verandah & listen to hammering & sawing. Bob and Mrs Taylor are giving up the village shop to the nephew & his bride, and making the Smithy into a groundfloor flat. [In 1908 Bob and his brother, John, had inherited the business of joiner, undertaker and shopkeeper on the death of their father, John Taylor (senior), 'the Dormouse' to whom *Ginger and Pickles* was dedicated. Now they were passing it on to their nephew Billy Kenyon. The shop closed during the Second World War.] I have always hoped against hope that a smith might turn up. It seems one applied, for 2 days a week; but Robert asked increased rent and F.Sat[terthwaite] asked a lot for fitments which will now be scrapped. Apart from inconvenience, I like to see a smithy. The nearest is Ambleside and he has more work than he can manage. Don't you hate changes? In these days one never knows what one may get up to find any morning. I am glad to hear in Hawkshead that Miss Goode's operation was fairly successful, though her sight will be somewhat affected, it is a calamity for anyone, and awfully sad for an artist. There is still beauty in the world to look at, though much that is annoying. I shall miss the Folk dancing I fear this spring. I enjoyed the book thank you [for] sending it.

With love yrs aff
Beatrix Heelis

I will re read Adam Bede, (skipping Dinah!)

Ten weeks after leaving hospital Beatrix had been rushed back again with suspected appendicitis but escaped another operation. She wrote to a young friend in late July, 'They kept me 9 days and then I came home by train'.

Sawrey
July 19th.39

Dear Miss Choyce,

I am interested to have the cutting of cactus, it may be like one that was in the cool greenhouse at Lindeth How – a very delicate salmon pink; growing something like the common magenta, but larger and much more lovely. I think it should root easily. Its been a season for cactus. I have had 2 plants large scarlet cactus with 6 flowers each – a blaze of flame colour.

Your news of the sale was tantalising, in a way – it will have been so to *you* if things go cheap – yet what is the old saying? what is not absolutely needed or not room for – is dear at a penny? I could not deal with the information which reached me in Liverpool – I had some digestive trouble and went back to hospital for a thorough overhaul. The surgeon was perfectly satisfied with the condition from the first operation – he said I might have been unwise (shall we say greedy!?) eating all manner of food too soon, during convalescence. I am more inclined to blame the weather. There was such extreme heat, followed by cold nights. At present it is muggy & thundery, the hay will be a slow job. We have only got one field, and another new cut. There was nothing to cut in June when the weather was fine. How short the corn is, I was looking at the fields along the line by Ormskirk and south Lancs. The thunderstorms had not laid the corn, it did not look 2 foot 6 inch high, and turning colour.

Things don't seem too good at all. That horrible monster just takes what he wants – whatever may happen about Dantzig [sic] – its pretty clear he has got Trieste and a Mediterranean port without any fighting; bullied Italy, and given her a free hand in the Tyrol as a sop [Hitler and Mussolini had signed a ten-year political and military alliance on 22 May].

I wonder whether your camp is full of militia. Liverpool was over shadowed by the Thetis inquiry. [The new British submarine, HMS *Thetis*, had sunk on 1 June after diving trials off Birkenhead, with 99 lives lost.] And possessed by Orange day processions; which passed off peaceably. I came home yesterday. It was a bother going, but much more satisfactory.

Miss Goode's cottage looks to be inhabited, I have not heard whether she is back.

Thunder again! There has been a climber struck by lightning & killed on the Coniston fells.

Vegetables have come on with a rush, and there is a good crop of black currants & rasps. Strawberries were good, only the birds were past keeping off them.

Miss Lobb has not long survived her friend. Perhaps it may be like the Severn's sale at Brantwood, where much was brought for a society which runs the house as a hostel of 'brotherhood' for teachers.

Thank you for the cutting I hope it may be lucky. I am very fond of cacti, and with half doz pots there are always two or more that flower – though the largest scarlet is only every 4th year.

With love yrs aff
Beatrix Heelis

Did I tell you the piano tuner says the piano wants some cleaning which could easily be done.

Beatrix, with Tzusee and Chuleh, photographed in 1936
by an American friend

On 31 August women and children were evacuated from London, and on 2 September the British National Service Bill meant the calling up of all men between the ages of 19 and 41. On 1 September Germany had invaded Poland and annexed Danzig and on 3 September Britain and France declared war on Germany.

Castle Cottage
Sawrey
Ambleside
Dec 9. 39

My dear Miss Choyce

I do not wonder that you find the times depressing, and lonely in the evenings – the blackout is making it dangerous to go out after dark; besides we get colds more easily as we grow older and find more difficulty in throwing them off. I am not quite sure whether I am beginning one myself; caught from Stevens in the car, he is a sniffler & snuffler in winter. We have just had enough petrol, by pooling our coupons(!) Mr Heelis has extra, owing to the Agricultural Committee, and Magistrate's clerk's work; and – so far – the lorry is not rationed. The long distance work is lessening now when sales are over. *Exasperating* they have been. The "grading" was off at Ulverston market on Thursday; until after Christmas there is decontrol. My last and *oldest* lot of fat draft ewes made 26/6, whereas much better sheep have been sold for 21/ to 23/-. If butcher's meat had ever been reasonable one would feel there was some compensation – but I think the profit has gone to profiteering dealers. At the large fairs it was remarked that there were scarcely any bidders. A few men have bought up the sheep and taken them away to other markets where the grading was higher. We don't want profiteering, but farmers deserve a little improvement in prices. Dairy cows, which are not controlled, are dear. The ploughing committees are more sensible than in the last war. It is admitted that this is a stock raising rather than a corn growing district. We could have harvested corn this autumn – but next autumn may be just as wet, and a crop wasted. I have 7 acres here & at Hawkshead field – the latter is 5 acres that were left under a poor root crop without seeding, and naturally never supported anything – except rabbits. Rabbits & Deer are a problem. Mr Heelis on the committee reports much discontent abt. "calling up" – the actual number of farm lads is very small, because there are scarcely any youths on the farms – they all go off to the slate quarries or to Barrow. But a few have been taken – the farmers are very sore, because when they consented to plough they understood their men would not be taken. It is a little difficult to say. The lads want to go. They regard the war as a pic-nic. I only trust and hope they won't be gassed. Hitler is an awful brute; and what a mad mistake to invite the Russians in. I think they are a rotten country, but the Allies have enough on hand; and apparently Sweden won't move till attacked herself.

I think there should be some official sharing out about ploughing. either the govt. plough & ploughmen like last time, or some directed pooling of local men. I have almost more than enough labour here, and had fortunately secured 2 young horses. So far we have worked with one neighbour, at Troutbeck: he setting out and directting [sic] and I supplying the 2 staggs [?horses]. I hope they are not taken off me! Mechanical traction is not very suitable up here.

The forms and circulars are much over done. What their clerking is like?? I put down to grow oats & potatoes, and I am being circularised to know why I object to grow an approved crop? As for retailer's licence – its past following up about butter. The same official who signed my licence says he cannot accept my registered consumers because "W. Heelis Hill Top Farm" does not appear to be licenced. If he writes again I shall ask him if he wants the address of the rabbit holes? I am licenced to sell milk butter potatoes rabbits and margarine!!!

Sometimes I regret the times when we weeded turnips and worked with our hands. Perhaps it is as well for my peace of mind that I am *decidedly* too old for manual work; there has been plenty to do, without trying to do what one has no longer strength for. The weather has been horrible lately. I wish it would dry up. One job I am very interested in – is the timber question – also smothered with official red tape. There is a great shortage of pit props, partly owing to increased demand for the iron ore mines; and partly interruption of cargoes from northern Europe. Its a pity to see fine young larch go down, prematurely cut; but its wanted. As regards the general question of cutting down trees – I think $\frac{1}{3}$ of the trees in this district could be felled with positive advantage to the landscape, provided they were properly selected, and the remaining trees left in suitable groups. So – on the few fine days – I go about with a paint pot – to be felled – and acorns to be dibbled in.

I am very well now; but aged [she was seventy-three]. W.H. has *not* been standing up well to the worries of the times. He got a bad chill & was in bed a week, which is unusual; he said he got it at the police station but he had been on very cold jobs inspecting ploughing land. The Agricultural Committee will be mainly indoor work in future, & he has given up special constable. He was on it for many years, with only twice out (for special shows at Barrow) now its too cold work for elderly, besides the driving in the dark. One clerk is called up, and another seriously ill, off work.

There are very few locals out, as yet. A contingent of ex-service are at Barrow. So far our local military are very quiet neighbours; I send them apples & newspapers – my only complaint is I have not got back sacks. The apples are keeping fairly well; but potatoes are very very bad. I am wondering if there will be enough seed potatoes next spring. One things certain, its little use planting extra "spuds" in our old black garden soil. The healthiest crop I had seen was on a patch of rough ground where the man had ploughed up & burnt bracken roots.

The piano tuner was in yesterday, he played pleasantly before leaving. The piano has the advantage of a fire as I have slept in that room since last spring. It would be nice to hear some dance music, but I doubt the wisdom of people leaving home before the turn of winter. I hope your brother won't be knocked up, it was good of him to come forward. Men are not always put to the jobs where they are the most use and most fit for. Is it not extraordinary & wrong that there are still people on the dole?

I wonder whether the lots of poultry and 15 pigs "is sound policy? The "cottager's pig" requires finishing with meal; but it makes use of some waste swill. There are none here; and no sign of revival – the sanitary inspectors did away with the pig styes; and I have no pleasure in a pig that is fed all wrong by people who won't feed as they are told, in reasonable quantity. The farms have not done so bad – I sold about 800 sheep! poor prices, but numerous.

Yrs aff
Beatrix Heelis

Its tiresome for you that you cannot get books; and no piano. I hope yr doctor gives you something to snuff up. I expect you have cattarrh [sic].

Soon after the outbreak of war Beatrix had answered a plea from her cousin, Ulla Hyde Parker, for a quiet refuge for her family. Her husband, Sir William Hyde Parker, Bt., was recovering from severe head injuries sustained in an accident in the blackout, and they had a son aged two and a daughter born on the day war was declared. Beatrix had allowed them to move in to her most precious house, Hill Top. The Government was starting to commandeer empty houses for those evacuated from highly populated areas.

Castle Cottage
Sawrey
Ambleside
May 8.41

My dear Miss Choyce

I hoped there might be a letter from you this morning, but letters take a long time – and go astray. I wrote last Sunday suggesting that you and Tom might like to come to Hill Top for a while – I don't say "for the duration" which no one can foresee; the length of your stay would depend upon whether you were occupied and happy – and no ructions – which evacs. [evacuees] occupy themselves with. Now, since I wrote, on Sunday night there was a bad raid near enough – never alarming – but I cannot say we are a 'safe' area. Still I think it would be much pleasanter than where you are? It would be a great pleasure to me to see you again – and frankly – (selfishly?) – I am concerned about the house [Hill Top] & contents. The Parkers went home to Suffolk this morning, having brought the car to fetch the children. Barrow has had painful raids, people are leaving. A few minutes ago I was rung up by a tired sad voice, three ladies arrived at Coniston – no where to go did I know of a cottage? She sounded like a lady – but goodness knows who might arrive & have to be admitted. I cannot keep it long empty. I am very aggravated about Belmount Hall, Miss Owen's old house, I bought it along with some land and it would hold a shoal of refugees, but the Forestry have taken it for landgirls; which is interesting and useful, but they are so awfully slow with red tape. They promised to have girls available by end of May; but they never get a start with new baths new cooker etc. etc. If I could have been sure of getting things I would have got it going in half the time. Brathay Hall near Ambleside is being "Waifs & Strays" – they are asking for volunteers. There is any amount of voluntary occupation, I don't know whether any paid – they are wanting billets for 4,000 for the new factory. I hope you and

Tom will be able to come and "hold the fort" and, if able later to do a little work, there would be opportunity! If I were not married I would go to Hill Top myself & give up this house; but W.H. is placid, he will never believe in scarcity of sugar or marmalade or arrival of evacs. until they are on the door step! Grange has been bombed, and a village south of here.

Yrs aff.

H.B. Heelis

There would be sufficient blankets linen & cutlery, for you two, parafin cooking stove, coal rather scarce, any quantity of wood.

If the fares are a difficulty I would forward notes by post.

From the two versions of the story THE CHINESE UMBRELLA *that Beatrix sent as 'Christmas letters', one to Alison Hart and one to Louie Choyce, in December 1942, we know that Louie and Tom Choyce did return to Hill Top. In Alison's story Beatrix wrote, 'Miss Louie Choyce is living in Tom Kitten's house with her brother Tom Choyce ... When I got to Brathay Hall – (where Miss Choyce dishwashes for the Waifs and Strays ...'. It is not known how long they stayed.*

[?]

May 26 43

Dear Miss Choyce,

I can imagine you working away! The spoiliation [sic] is lamentable but there is some satisfaction for you in working in a place where there is soil. Walter has been tidying the grass round Hill Top front; but really that bed is not worth setting, although I have plenty of sprouts etc. Strange to say my enormous brocoli [sic] plants have flowered, very good tasty cauliflowers, several very large though I threw away the largest plants in dispair [sic] – at least I let Miss Hammond use them for rabbits. They are 18 months old! There has been another wet day, it did no end of good, every ones turnips were going off with fly, and we had just re sown so I hope this next lot will do better; mangolds were up and frosted. If *you* had chickens at Hill Top you would be "in a taking." Mrs Storey set 2 hens with eggs from Troutbeck for herself & me which hatched 21. but six have been taken by jackdaws – I suspected rats or a hawk till Wellan actually saw a jackdaw fly off with a brown Rhodey [Rhode Island Red] chick in its bill – I hope a cockerell [sic] – most aggravating. A jackdaw has been shot &

hung up, the hens & surviving chicks are on the lamb-calf grass next drying ground. It seems as safe as anywhere, I could only put them in Bull Banks, on account of corn & hay. The hay grass looks very forward, but except seeds – I doubt if it is as forward as it looks. There is wild oats, a most rubbishy grass which comes early & seeds itself again, before other grasses are ready to cut. The news is an exciting pause – where and when? Both the Burns's sons in law are safe. We heard considerable thumps one evening, but don't know whether it was on northeast coast, or practice fire in the twilight. The birds sing nearly all night. The country is lovely just now, the hawthorns so sweet, the air is full of their scent. The rhodendrons [sic] are better than usual thanks to the rain. You will be amused to hear all us unlawabiding inhabitants are on strike. Fancy being instructed to *go* to the Ulverston food office for new ration books – 16 miles & no bus. I found [they had] got to the Cs when I heard not one person had gone. Mr H and Mrs R. (different days) are defiant. The Grasmere A B C. have gone to Windermere but then there are buses though I'm told many are left standing as they are full before reaching Ambleside – what a silly trick. Our peas are just ready to come into flower. With love to you and Mr Thomas

yrs aff

Beatrix Heelis

I go in [to Hill Top] mournfully and water plants, I must take a duster, where *does* it come from?

Castle Cottage
Sawrey
June 29.43

My dear Miss Choyce

I am indeed sorry to hear of *shingles*; its an aggraviting [sic] complaint, and bad to get completely clear of. The only consolation is that its better to come out – instead of suppressed gout. I don't know whether hot weather is good for it. Its *hot* here, suddenly – perfect hay weather, cloudless blue sky and a nice breeze. We held back during the cold showers and only started on Saturday. Crops seem fairly heavy; this belated warm weather will help the later fields. Potatoes and all have grown slowly and spindled through want of sun. We are just starting new potatoes – not particularly tasty – Duke of Yorks – yellow and rather mealy. Peas are nearly ready. The fruit crop – non est! deplorable! there were very few blossoms after the bullfinch devastation, and then there was a late frost. I have put the net on the blackcurrants at Hill Top. There seem to be no plums at all. I think I will take the opportunity to cut back the tree, later on.

We are like to be a laughing stock with machinery. The combine Austin motor mower has been behaving badly; and this morning when it seemed to be working decently in the P.O meadow one wheel sank into a drain. Geoff fetched the Fordson tractor to pull it out. It mows twice as fast as the horses *when* it will go. Two mares are carting this afternoon and the third is looking after the 3 foals.

The garden here is very gay; white bell flowers everywhere amongst the weeds, and the house covered with roses. The pinks are very full – I have been excited about your cactus, it has had 5 flowers – lovely – very like my old pink cactus, but prettier as the trumpet is pearly white instead of deep pink all over. It is such a pretty plant, with fresh green leafage. One of my scarlet has had 7 large flowers; the other variety at Hill Top has had only one flower, it does not flower so freely as the pink. I have planted out sprouts & autumn cauliflowers, and plenty of lettuce to come on. No prospect of poor Tom Christie this season; the doctors begin to say there may be a diseased bone in his hand which may require scraping. He has been in hospital nearly 4 months. We keep very well here, and enjoying the change of weather. The news is – suspence [sic] – I wonder if the unhappy European nations will have strength to rise, when deliverance comes. We hear the bombers going over and back every night nearly.

Miss Brownlow has just been in to see about Guides Camp – rather complaining of the Education Authorities who have 'staggered' the holidays in such a way that half the 60 children cannot come. I hope you will be able to give a better acct of yourself next letter. You want Woodfall Spa [?Woodfield Spa Water]. How is Tom keeping? Tell him it really *can* be fine & hot at Sawrey now he has gone away. It will probably end in thunder.

With love yrs aff.
Beatrix Heelis

By this time in the war there was strict paper rationing and letters were written on whatever scrap paper came to hand. This letter was written on pages torn from an old account book.

Sawrey
August 16.43

My dear Miss Choyce,

We are having most unpleasant weather, usually bitterly cold at night, at this moment stuffy warm – but always heavy showers. Aug 18th. I began to write 2 days ago but there is no improvement – very thundery and sopping under the corn. Two farmers have had the binder. I think it is foolishness, so long as the oats stand up. Ours is ripe in patches; scarcely ready. Its a wet August. There has only been one rain big enough to raise the [River] Brathay, but its never dry. Mr. G. Aitcheson [sic] died last Sunday. He was only 6–62, what a waster he has been of life & health since he was a good looking young man – said to have steadied of recent years, but a martyr to asthma.

The war news is very encouraging. How the poor occupied countries must be longing for rescue – they will all be dead of hunger if it does not come before winter. I would like to see Russia conquer Germany at home; modern warfare is no job for civilized nations; their offer to make Rome an open city is a clever try-on, they will just try to change Hitler and wriggle out if they can get round the Americans. Talk of wriggling out – this further call up of young women has not combed any more out of Sawrey. I can't think how they escape? Our potatoes are very bad in the garden, a poor crop and a lot are more like corals? or starfish? Not rotten, and the tops although spindled are green; but instead of ⬭ ⬭ ⬭ there are things like this underground, some in the vegetable garden on comparatively new soil. I must get rid of all seed and have it limed when we have a waggon. The garden is very overgrown. I can't get at it with the wet; the phloxes will soon be over, & summer also – a short summer. How the days have drawn in, with the clock. [During the Second World War, Daylight Saving Time (when the clocks are put forward one hour) operated from1941 to 1944, with Double Summer Time (two hours) during the summer.] The blackout still enforced. Raids seem pretty bad in some places, a family named Fothergill, with Ambleside connections, were caught at a cinema in a town somewhere South. They had celebrated a golden wedding, and the old lady & 4 daughters went to the pictures – she & 2 married daughters killed; and it is said in Ambleside that *130* were killed at same place – which is not in newspapers so we will hope untrue.

I have managed to buy 6lbs of "best desert Victorias" from Miss Short at 9d. You never saw such plums, thinnings, with about a dozen decent ones amongst! however the jam is good. There will be vegetable marrows & blackberries, nothing else – except I have bespoken some honey; old Mr Stables Mrs Walker's father has a good crop, I wonder how Dr Allen's bees have done. Wellan has just come in for his 10 o'clock, he says they had a good view from the Post – he thinks they saw a plane brought down, a red ball falling from the sky. I heard a lot of planes & noise, but did not look out, probably Merseyside or N Wales. Its about time it ended.

I hope you & Tom keep well. I have had a bit of cold with the change from heat to chilly nights, but its going. I went to Hill Top & had a good dust last week.

Whenever it dries up I will take Walter & have a trimming outside. There seem to be a good few apples on the Worcester pe[a]rmains. I wish it had been on any other, for they don't keep long, & the birds will be savage on them if left to ripen. None on the crab or the Quar[r]enden. To crown all – a piebald hutch rabbit has been loose in this garden – she was rescued unhurt from the jaws of the Pekes, but she had done some nibbling, especially choosing cauliflowers!

With love yrs aff
Beatrix Heelis

Your cactus has grown another (6th) flower bud. I am trying a cutting from it; its a most pleasing variety.

Castle Cottage
Sawrey
Ambleside
Sept 17.43

My dear Miss Choyce

How pleasing to know that the Morris paper has helped to refresh Tuck Mill [Louie Choyce's home]. It is shocking to feel that the firm of William Morris has gone. But its influence still lives; the Society for Preservation of Ancient Buildings is his best memorial. Although they have not been able

to save enough, that Society has enormously educated taste in "resto-
ration". The Victorian architects and clergy did more mischief than
Hitler. As you talk of Weeds – you have had rain? but not like here! its been
something awful, just like 1919. There were 2 days without rain in August
and 1½ days in September. We got 17 carts of oats on the last fine spell.
Lots of oats are uncut yet and sprouting badly. We got the Castle field only
– many farms have got none yet. It has been less wet on the Cumberland
coast. I hear from Jennie [sic] Mackereth it is nearly all carried about
Maryport. There has been constant high wet winds from the sea, turning
to heavy showers when the clouds hit the fells. Two very loud thunderstorms last Monday Tues. nights and torrents of rain. I have been bothered with a bronchial cough for more than a fortnight and very tired of it, as
it keeps me awake at nights, it is just the weather prevents me from
throwing it off. We have picked one basketful of apples and there may be 3
baskets more. A lot of them won't keep either. There has been a great crop
of blackberries, and I have ordered ½ score of damsons from Agnes Pos's
relations in Crosthwaite, and there are marrows, so we are alright for jam.
The garden would have been alright but there have been 2 rabbits – one a
tame black & white – it did eat a lot before the pekes obligingly caught and
held it. Cauliflowers seemed its favourite food. I hear there is a new matron
at Brathay [Hall] – no particulars. Mrs J. Fowkes was here yesterday,
asking after you; she says they got their corn well at Wallington. I hope
Tom will get back weight, I am taking cod maltine. I want to get right
before Mrs Edwards lands up next week, she is coming for 2 nights,
between posts, she is booked up for relief jobs till New Year, there seems a
great shortage of midwives. The war news is very interesting, how splendid
the Russian advance. I hope our wet weather does not spread to Ukraine –
it would be a good job if they can drive the Germans over the Dnieper
before all is stopped by autumn rains and mud. *Never* did I see such
tiresome showers, they had the sheaves spread out in a gleam of sunshine
yesterday afternoon but before a cart could be got it was raining in
torrents. The farmers in the Yorkshire dales are in revolt abt next season's
ploughing; its nonsense amongst hills. The lamb sales are coming on; sent
50 to Broughton, 15 smallest made 9/ each which is not very grand! I wish
we might have been permitted a hot pot or Scotch broth!! I wish I could
help you to matting. I doubt if there is any worth while at Belmount and I
don't know your station, its not size for posting.

With love yrs aff.
Beatrix Heelis

Castle Cottage
Sawrey
Ambleside
Nov 30th.43

My dear Miss Choyce,

You said you were intending to go to Bournemouth, should I send off that piece of carpet, or wait till after Christmas? I could easily get it to the station by Bruce Dixon any time? I must tell you it has had moths in it, but I don't think you need be afraid of it, when Walter has had it out in the yard here & he gave it a good hard beating in. Anyway it would be safe to use short loose lengths on a bare floor. What a price carpets are now! I don't know if you ever saw a green axminster carpet, which I bought for this dining room. It proved unsuitable, showed every mark, and when Lindeth How was cleared I kept the Persian carpet instead, and took the Axminster to the spare bedroom, which it was too good for, besides being under the heavy wardrobe; then I tried it at Hill Top and it made the oil paintings look *yellow* – in short it was a White Elephant, and I was afraid of moths, rolled up. It cost £30 at Storey's, Kensington High Street. I sent it to a sale recently and it made £52. Mr McVey had a sale at Ambleside, including some surplus things of Miss Hough's & Mrs Aitcheson's [sic]. I have not heard any news of Brathay [Hall] lately. I hear Mrs Green = Mollie Byers has got tired of going, and has got a paid job at the Ferry school which counts as war work – not many stuck it like you did! I do hope your sister has not stuck to work too long. By your account she must have been very much over doing it. It will be nice for you & Tom to be able to get to Bournemouth occasionally. Nancy has been here for part of her week's holiday, looking well, and enjoying her outdoor farm work, she asked after you. I am still rather under the weather. We had some really fine dry frosts, but I was disappointed to find I was not ready to stand the cold – it was really severe frost – so I got a cough again, but it did not last long. Today has been pleasant sunshine. I have been pruning creepers against the wall in the sun here. Walter did the japonica against Hill Top. Nancy & I went across & had a rummage round, taking somethings there & bringing some back – which would amuse you. I brought the spreaders off the Valor perfection [paraffin oil stove]. I have no intention of unlocking if I can help it; but there is always risk of having to if the water works bust up. Nancy put a hasp & padlock on the door of the china room. Its a problem. One thing's certain; its no time to change servants if avoidable. Those females are the limit. Mrs Rogerson seems much better and she is looking forward to a holiday, going to Manchester for a week to visit Sally Benson. Mrs Edwards is here for a "rest", and says she will manage with the outside help coming in. She has had rather a hard summer and a heavy fall, nothing broken but bruised – a child threw something & a dog ran under her legs. She will be here into New Year – so I will be looked after if I am ill – rather more than enough!! We all have to grow old; but some of us don't take to stopping in. I don't know that there is much news. Mrs Spencer the Vicar's wife is dead poor woman; also Mrs Penny at Eeswyke. The hills have been snow down to the foot & hail showers here. Very little ploughing done yet – land too sticky for the Fordson & the horses running out still. We have had the threshing machine – the oats came out rather well, but of course there was awful waste. The fields just grew as green as if sown with winter oats, that was with standing too long over ripe.

Let me know about sending the carpet – to Strivinham [Shrivenham] Station. GWR [Great Western Railway]?

Love from yrs aff.
Beatrix Heelis

The war news is heartening – but rather horrid??

And I had a letter from an old servant in Earlscourt who says she was pinned under her bed for 2 hrs and the flat on fire! quite recently.

Beatrix Potter did not recover from this last illness and died in Castle Cottage on the night of 22 December 1943, aged seventy-seven. Her death certificate, signed by Dr A. Brownlie, gave the cause of death as 'acute bronchitis, myocarditis, and carcinoma of the uterus'.

Louie Choyce died on 30 December 1963 at the age of eighty-seven.

INDEX

THE BEATRIX POTTER SOCIETY

The Beatrix Potter Society was founded in 1980 by a group of people professionally involved in the curatorship of Beatrix Potter material. It exists to promote the study and appreciation of the life and works of Beatrix Potter (1866–1943), who was not only the author and illustrator of *The Tale of Peter Rabbit* and other classics of children's literature, but also a landscape and natural history artist, diarist, farmer and conservationist – in the latter capacity she was responsible for the preservation of large areas of the Lake District through her gifts to the National Trust.

The Society is a registered charity and its membership is worldwide. Its activities include regular talks and meetings in London and visits to places connected with Beatrix Potter. An annual Linder Memorial Lecture is given each spring to commemorate the contribution made to Beatrix Potter studies by Leslie Linder and his sister Enid. The first of these was given at the Victoria and Albert Museum by Margaret Lane, as Patron of the Society. Biennial Study Conferences are held in the Lake District and Scotland and are attended by members from around the world.

A quarterly Newsletter, issued free to members, contains articles on a wide range of topics as well as information about meetings and visits, reviews of books and exhibitions, members' letters, and news of Beatrix Potter collections both in the United Kingdom and elsewhere. The Society also publishes the proceedings of its Study Conferences and various occasional papers.

For further information write to: The Membership Secretary, High Banks, Stoneborough Lane, Budleigh Salterton, Devon, EX9 6HL.